INFANTRY UNIFORMS

INCLUDING ARTILLERY AND OTHER SUPPORTING CORPS OF BRITAIN AND THE COMMONWEALTH
1855–1939

INFANTRY UNIFORMS

INCLUDING ARTILLERY AND OTHER
SUPPORTING CORPS OF BRITAIN AND
THE COMMONWEALTH
1855–1939

in colour

by
ROBERT and CHRISTOPHER
WILKINSON-LATHAM

Illustrated by
JACK CASSIN-SCOTT
The Notes on Weapons specially written for this
Volume by Major John Wilkinson-Latham

BLANDFORD PRESS
Poole   Dorset

First published 1970
Illustrations Copyright © 1970 Blandford Press
Text Copyright © 1970 R. & C. WILKINSON-LATHAM
Notes on Weapons © 1970 MAJOR J. WILKINSON-LATHAM

Reprinted 1976

ISBN 0 7137 0525 6

Colour printed in Great Britain by Cowells of Ipswich
Text set in Monotype Times New Roman, printed and bound in Great
Britain by Richard Clay (The Chaucer Press), Ltd., Bungay, Suffolk

CONTENTS

PREFACE

This is a companion volume to *Infantry Uniforms of Britain and the Commonwealth 1742–1855*, and covers the development of uniform, weapons and equipment up to 1939. It follows a similar pattern to the first volume, except that the individual vignettes have been assembled at the end of the book instead of on the Uniform plate. We have devoted eighty-nine plates to uniforms and seven to weapons, shakos and medals. We now include two principal figures on each plate rather than one in the foreground and one in the background as in the previous volume.

We have used contemporary photographs, as far as possible, for information to show what was actually worn rather than what was prescribed to be worn, and we have inspected and noted many of the items of dress depicted in the plates.

The text matter follows the pattern of the earlier book, and we hope that it will appeal to the model maker, the military artist, the military collector and to all those interested in military pageantry who wish to know more about the colourful history and traditions of the Infantry of Britain and the Commonwealth.

We are grateful to those who have helped in the accumulation of the facts and information used. Our thanks too to our mother, who was a source of encouragement in the preparation of this volume.

ROBERT WILKINSON-LATHAM
CHRISTOPHER WILKINSON-LATHAM

Cannes, 06,
France

INTRODUCTION

When man first joined together with his fellows to fight in groups, either to hold his territory against others or to gain more for himself, he fought dismounted and with close combat weapons. Since that time, the brunt of all fighting has been borne by the man on foot, the infantryman.

Despite the sophistication of modern warfare, it is still the foot soldier who is in the forefront of the battle and finally gets to grips with his opposite number. The main changes that have taken place in the infantry battle are those that concern not only the uniform and weapons but also the mode of arrival in the fighting zone.

Originally, the footslogger, as he came to be known, marched into battle carrying everything he needed on his person and then, with the advent of horse-drawn transport, his heavier equipment was brought up behind him in the wagons. Later still towards the end of the nineteenth century, there came into being the Mounted Infantry, who rode their horses to the battle area and then dismounted to fight in the traditional role of the foot soldier.

The First World War introduced motor transport, but due to the type of terrain this was not of much practical use, and the Infantryman was back on his feet again, carrying on his broad back all the necessities of life, as on the Somme in 1916, when the assaulting troops went into battle carrying their rifles and bayonets, 200 rounds of ammunition, a valise, small pack, water-bottle, grenades, pick or shovel, blanket and rations with a total weight of nearly three-quarters of a hundredweight.

The Second World War introduced many more methods by which the Infantryman and even the supporting troops could arrive at the scene of a battle. There was the lorry-borne Infantry of the Armoured Divisions, which soon became armoured in their own right by the introduction of armoured personnel carriers. The parachute, used originally by soldiers for escaping from balloons, was brought into service as a means of creating new fighting zones by allowing quantities of men and materials to be dropped in comparative secrecy behind the enemy lines. Large gliders, seating up to thirty men, were employed to crash land either in the line or behind it, as the Germans did when they assaulted the Low Countries in 1940. Now that the helicopter has reached its advanced state of development, it, too, is used to ferry men and equipment into the heart of the fighting area.

The period covered by this book, 1855–1939, brought about hundreds of changes, both major and minor, in the dress and uniforms of the Infantry soldier of both Britain and the Commonwealth, and every effort has been made to illustrate and describe these. Khaki, which in Indian vernacular means 'of earth or dust colour', was introduced at the time of the Indian Mutiny, by staining the white drill uniforms with tea so that the soldiers would appear less visible against the sun-baked rocks of the Indian plains and mountain ranges. Similarly, the green of rifle regiments owes its origin to the 60th or King's Royal Rifles when fighting against the French in the heavily wooded country that was the frontier of the New England colonies.

The use of scarlet or red as a military colour dates from the days of King Charles II when the Royal Army was reorganised and it was decided that they should adopt the colours of the Royal livery, i.e. red with blue facings.

Regimental customs and traditions have always played a very important part in the life of the British Army and never more so than in the Infantry, where every man who serves or who has served in a particular regiment remembers with pride its own customs and the days in the regimental calendar that take note of special occasions in the long history of that unit.

The Royal Berkshire Regiment captured a Russian side drum in the Crimea, and since that time officers and their guests at weekly guest nights have been 'rolled' into mess by the orderly drummer playing rolls on that original trophy. Incidentally, the regiment repeated the exercise by capturing a German side drum in the First World War.

In the days when wigs and long hair were worn by soldiers it was customary for the tail or queue to be tied with ribbon at the nape of the neck. In 1808 wigs and queues were abolished and hair was ordered to be cut short, but the Royal Welch Fusiliers, who were at that time in Nova Scotia, did not receive the order, and consequently continued to wear this order of dress. This fact is commemorated by the right to wear a black ribboned flash on the back of the uniform collar by all members of the regiment.

In the fifteenth century part of the armour was the gorget or throat protector. When armour went into decline with the general introduction of firearms the gorget remained as a decorative part of the officers' uniform. This finally went out of favour with the authorities, and all that is left are the cords and buttons from which it would have been suspended, and then only on the collars of general officers and officers of the Oxfordshire and Buckinghamshire Light Infantry, the last regiment to receive the order which abolished their wear.

Regimental mottoes are also the subject of much pride and are derived from many sources. The Gordon Highlanders, whose badge is that of the Marquis of Huntley, have adopted his motto *Bydand* meaning 'Onwards', while the Dorsetshire Regiment were granted the motto *Primus in Indus* to commemorate the distinguished conduct of the old 39th Foot at the battle of Plassey in 1757. *Celer et Audax* borne by the 60th Rifles was granted to them for their outstanding services in North America under General Wolfe, 1759.

Regimental badges, a study in themselves, also portray facets of regimental history. The Queen's Royal Regiment and the Worcestershire Regiment incorporate the Naval crown and the words '1st June 1794' in their badges, thus denoting their gallant conduct, when detachments of both Regiments served with the Navy under Lord Howe in his victory over the French at Brest.

The wreath on the colours, known as the 'Wreath of Immortelles', borne by the 24th Foot, The South Wales Borderers, was granted to them by Queen Victoria as a reward for their brave services in the Zulu War of 1879, the 1st Battalion being decimated at Isandhlwana and a detachment of the 2nd Battalion holding the post at Rorke's Drift against tremendous forces of Zulus.

On the anniversary of the battle of Minden, 1 August 1759,

the 12th, 20th, 25th, 37th and 51st Regiments of Foot celebrate their presence at the battle by wearing roses in their caps and decorating their drums and colours with roses. The exception is the 23rd Foot, the Royal Welch Fusiliers, who although present do not commemorate their exploits.

When the 'Iron Duke', His Grace the Duke of Wellington, lived at Apsley House at London's Hyde Park Corner, the regiments of Foot Guards made a custom of marching to attention as they passed his residence on the way to their duties. He was Colonel of the Grenadier Guards from 1827 to 1852, and in memory of this great man this small but distinctive ceremony is still observed by the Grenadier Guards.

The full story of the Infantry of the British Army and the Commonwealth may never be told and could not be, certainly, in one small volume. In this book we have endeavoured to portray the panoply of uniforms that were worn and give the reader an insight into the glory that was, and always will be, the Infantry of the British Army and its Commonwealth counterpart.

NOTE

The colour plates and the descriptive text which follows have been placed in date order and not in order of seniority. Where there coincides more than one regiment at any particular date, the following order of precedence has been adopted:

Royal Artillery
Royal Engineers
Foot Guards
Infantry of the Line
Corps
Volunteers, Militia, Territorials
Dominion and Commonwealth Troops

In the description of the coats and tunics, scarlet has been used for officers, and in the earlier section until 1871 (when scarlet was adopted for all other ranks) red for other ranks, although the colour worn by sergeants and above was more scarlet than red.

1 **53rd Foot.** Proposed Dress Officer *(centre)* and Privates
1855

2　**12th Foot**. Officers 1855

3   **23rd Foot.** Officer *(right)* and Private 1855

4 **93rd Foot.** Highlanders, Officer and NCO 1857

5 **95th Foot.** Officer and Private 1857

6 **55th Foot.** Officer and Private 1859

7 **31st Foot.** Officer and Private 1860

8/9 79th Foot. Officer. Private, Colour Sergeant and
Piper 1860

10 **32nd Middlesex Rifle Volunteers.** Privates 1860

11 **41st Middlesex (Enfield Lock) Rifle Volunteers.**
Officer and Private 1860

12 **77th Foot.** Private and Bandsman 1862

13　**General Officer.** 1865

14   **Royal Artillery.** Gunner 1865

15 **26th Foot**. Sergeant and Private 1866

16 **68th Foot**. Officers *(right)* and Sergeant 1868

17 **Royal Engineers.** Officer *(right)* and Sapper 1869

18 **18th Foot.** Officer *(right)* and Drummer 1869

19 **Royal Artillery.** Officer 1870

20   **Royal Engineers.** Officers 1874

21 **4th Foot.** Private and Bandsman 1875

22 **24th Foot.** Sergeant *(right)* and Private 1879

23 **29th Foot**. Officer *(right)* and Private 1879

24/25 **24th Foot** Colour Party 1880

26　**Royal Artillery.** Officers 1881

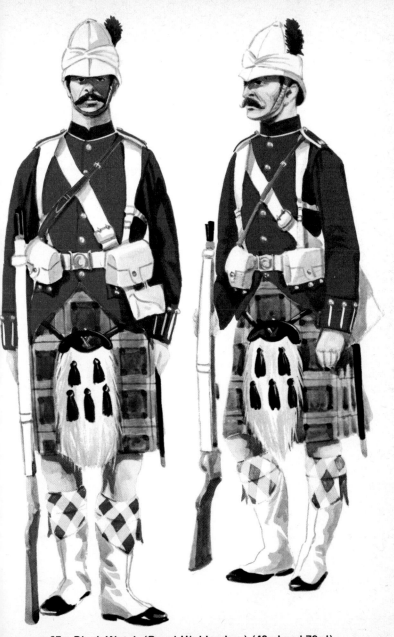

27 **Black Watch (Royal Highlanders) (42nd and 73rd).**
Privates 1882

28 3rd Middlesex Rifle Volunteers. Privates 1882

29 **Royal Inniskilling Fusiliers (27th and 108th).**
R.S.M. *(right)* and Drum Major 1884

30   **Princess Louise's (Argyll and Sutherland Highlanders)
(91st and 93rd).** Officers 1885

31   **1st Volunteer Battalion Royal Sussex Regiment.**
Sergeant *(right)* and Corporal 1886

32 **1st West Yorkshire Volunteer Artillery.** Officer *(right)*
and Gunner 1887

33 **1st Lanarkshire Rifle Volunteers.** Officer *(right)*
and Sergeant 1887

34　**Royal Military College.** Cadets 1889

35 **Royal Military Academy.** Cadets 1889

36 **Royal Scots Fusiliers (21st).** R.S.M. and Private 1890

37 1st London Rifle Volunteers (London Rifle Brigade).
Privates 1890

38 **1st Battalion Grenadier Guards.** Pioneers 1891

39 **Royal Welch Fusiliers (23rd).** R.S.M. *(right)* and
Private 1891

40/41 **3rd London Rifle Volunteers.** Officer and Privates 1891

42 **Royal Niger Hausas.** Privates 1891

43 **1st West India Regiment.** Sergeant *(right)* and Private
1892

44   **10th Battalion Royal Grenadiers.** Sergeant and
Staff Sergeant 1892

45   Princess of Wales' Own (Yorkshire Regiment) (19th).
Privates 1893

46 **7th Middlesex (London Scottish) Rifle Volunteers.**
Drum Major 1893

47 **13th Middlesex Volunteers Queen's Westminsters.**
Sergeant and Cyclist 1893

48 **Queen's Own Corps of Madras Sappers and Miners.**
Havildar *(right)* and Sapper 1893

49 **30th Punjab Infantry.** Havildar Major *(right)* and
Havildar 1894

50   **3rd Battalion Grenadier Guards.** Guardsmen 1895

51 **Royal Malta Artillery.** Officer *(right)* and Gunner 1895

52 **Cameronians (Scottish Rifles) (26th and 90th).**
Officer and Private 1896

53 **New South Wales Field Artillery.** Officer and Gunner 1896

54 **Victoria Infantry Brigade.** Officer and Private 1896

55 **East Lancashire Regiment (30th and 59th).**
Private and Ammunition Mule 1897

56/57 'A' Field Battery Royal Canadian Artillery. Gunners 1897

58 **Coldstream Guards.** Guardsman 1898

59 **Pacific Railway Militia.** Privates 1898

60 **Suffolk Regiment (12th)**. Privates 1899

61 **Military Foot Police.** Staff Sergeant and Corporal 1904

62 **Northamptonshire Regiment (48th and 58th).**
Officer and Bugler 1906

63　**2nd Prince of Wales' Own Gurkha Rifles (The Sirmoor Rifles).**
Subadar-Major and Rifleman 1906

64 **Honourable Artillery Company (Infantry).** Officer and Private 1909

65   **10th (Scottish) Battalion The King's (Liverpool)
Regiment.** Officer *(right)* and Sergeant 1909

66 **Royal Army Medical Corps.** Warrant Officer
Class II *(right)* and Orderly 1910

67 **Army Pay Corps.** Sergeant and Private 1910

68 **4th Battalion The Royal Scots (Lothian Regiment).**
Sergeant *(right)* and Bugler 1910

69　**15th Ludhiana Sikhs.** Colour Party 1910

70 **101st Grenadiers.** Bugler and Sepoys 1910

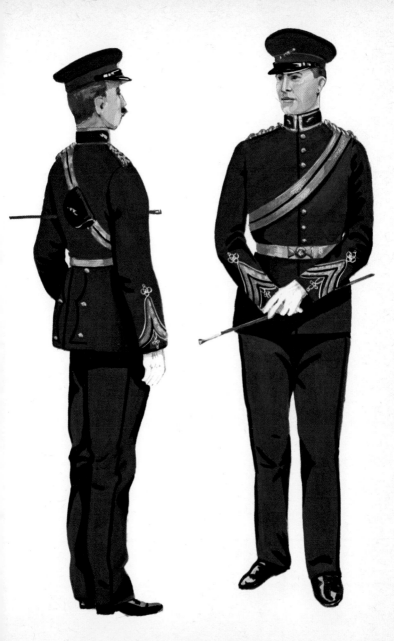

71 **Army Motor Reserve.** Officers 1911

72/73 **Royal Scots Fusiliers (21st).** Colour Party 1912

74 **Royal Flying Corps.** Officer and Sergeant 1913

75 **Royal Scots (Lothian Regiment) (1st).**
Officer *(right)* and Bugler 1914

76 **Highland Light Infantry (71st and 74th).**
Officer *(right)* and R.S.M. 1914

77 **Royal Irish Rifles (83rd and 86th).** Sergeant and Rifleman 1914

78　**Field Marshal Earl Kitchener of Khartoum** 1915

79　**Lancashire Fusiliers (20th).** Privates 1915

80 **East Surrey Regiment (31st and 70th).** Sergeant and Private 1917

81 **Seaforth Highlanders (Ross-shire Buffs, The Duke of Albany's) (72nd and 78th).** R.S.M. and Private 1917

82 **Royal Artillery.** Gunners 1918

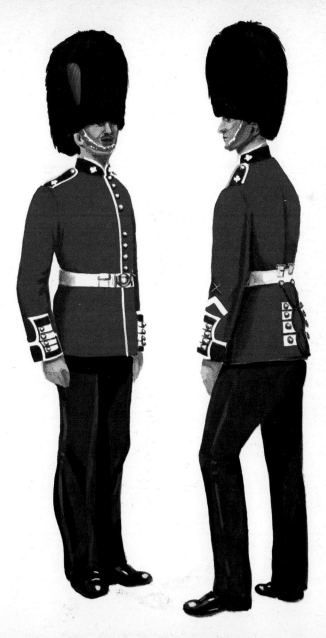

83 **Irish Guards.** Guardsmen 1934

84 **4th Battalion 1st Punjab Regiment.** Subadar *(right)*
and Sepoy 1934

85   **The Leicestershire Regiment (17th).** R.S.M. *(right)*
and Private 1937

86 **Royal Bombay Sappers and Miners.** Drum Major *(right)* and Drummer 1937

87 **The Queen's Royal Regiment (West Surrey) (2nd).**
Privates 1938

88/89   **The Middlesex Regiment (Duke of Cambridge's Own)
(57th and 77th).**
Vickers Machine-gun Demonstration Section 1939

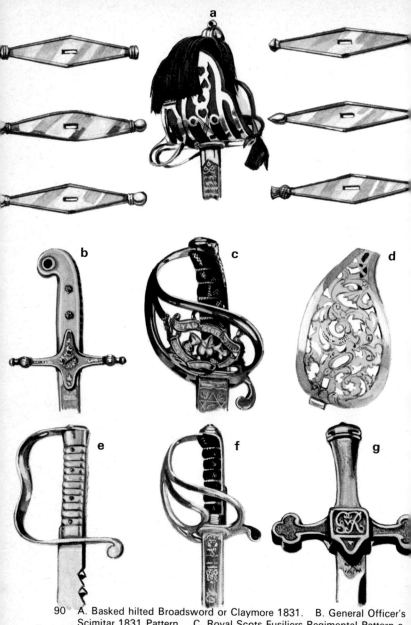

90   A. Basked hilted Broadsword or Claymore 1831.   B. General Officer's Scimitar 1831 Pattern.   C. Royal Scots Fusiliers Regimental Pattern c. 1870.   D. Royal Engineers 1856 Pattern.   E. Pioneer's Hanger 1856 Pattern.   F. Royal Artillery.   G. Bandsman's Sword 1895 Pattern.

1857–1901

1901–1910

1936–1952

b

h

Cameronians

c

Rifles

g

Grenadier Guards

d

Queen Victoria's Rifles

f

Indian Army

e

East India Company

a

91   Infantry Officers' Swords

92 A. The Victoria Cross. B. Crimea Medal (reverse). C. Obverse of Crimea Medal and Indian Mutiny Medal. D. Indian Mutiny Medal (reverse). E. Reverse of Third China War Medal 1900. F. Obverse of Queen's South Africa Medal and Third China War Medal 1900. G. Queen's South Africa Medal (reverse). H. The Military Cross.

a 1855–1869

b 1855–1869

c 1869–1878

d 1878–1881

e 1881–1908
(Volunteers)

f 1901–1939

93 Shako and Helmet Plates

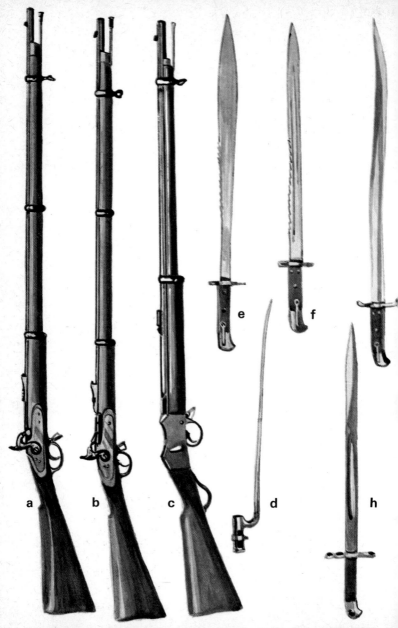

94 A. The Enfield Rifle 1853 Pattern. B. The Snider-Enfield Rifle 1867.
C. The Martini-Henry Rifle 1871. D/F. Bayonets as referred to in text.

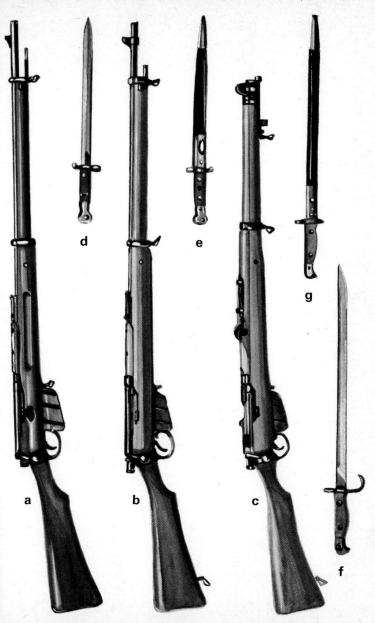

95 A. The Lee-Metford Rifle 1887. B. and C. The Lee-Enfield Rifle 1895. D/F. Bayonets as referred to in text.

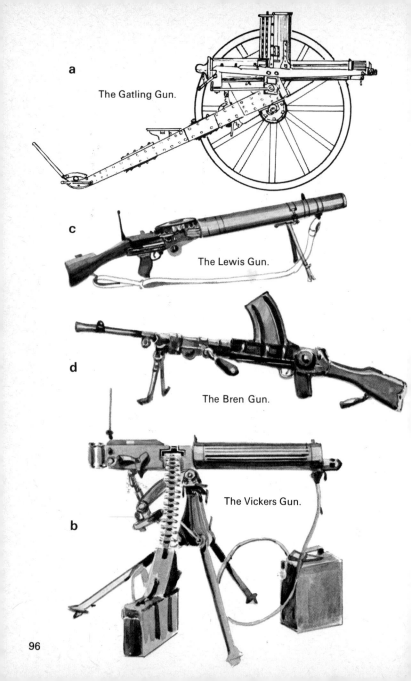

a

The Gatling Gun.

c

The Lewis Gun.

d

The Bren Gun.

The Vickers Gun.

b

96

1. 53rd Foot. Proposed Dress. Officer and Private, 1855

Head Dress

The head dress shown is illustrated in *History of the Dress of the British Soldier*, by Lieutenant-Colonel John Luard, published in 1852. The uniform and head dress never existed, and the illustration is based on material from that book. The helmet was shaped as shown, and it was stated: 'The helmet would sit firmly on the head, without top weight; it is high enough to prevent concussion from a blow and to admit sufficient air within; it may be black with brass ornaments (as shown), or with bronze ornaments, or made of any colour. Steel is too troublesome to keep clean, and too hot for tropical climates.'

Uniform

The other ranks' tunic proposed was of red cloth, double-breasted, and with round cuffs. Cuffs were to be edged around the top in tape and to have 3 buttons. Collar and shoulder straps were of the face colour and edged in tape. Trousers were grey with a broad yellow stripe down the outer seam of each leg. Spats were to be worn. The officer's uniform was similar.

Accoutrements

'A broad leather belt should be worn around the waist, to which the pouch could be attached by a runner, so that it can at leisure be brought to the front or rear. Both the belt and the pouch must be constructed for the purpose. The bayonet at present is hung on the left side; but it admits of a doubt if the method now practised of fixing is the best; it is possible that it would be more readily fixed and unfixed, and returned to its scabbard, if suspended on the right side; if so, the pouch could pass from the rear to the front, and back again, as easily on the other side. The man in marching order is represented with the strap across the chest, as at present worn, but it is very desirable that some better method of carrying the knapsack should be invented, as the strap above mentioned is found to be very painful to the chest.' (*Luard*)

Officers were still to retain the crossbelt with ornamental plate and to wear a sash around the waist.

Historical Note

As mentioned above, the descriptions have been taken from *History of the Dress of the British Soldier*. In the section on proposed dress and reformation Luard writes:

'For thirty-six years we have been reposing on the laurels gained at Waterloo, and have since then rather blinked at military improvements; while on the Continent they have been alive to every new invention.'

About the only proposed item adopted was the double-breasted tunic, and that for just one year.

2. 12th Foot. Officers, 1855

Head Dress

The Albert pattern shako was made obsolete on 16 January 1855 by the introduction of the second pattern shako. This measured $5\frac{1}{4}$ in. high in the front and $7\frac{1}{8}$ in. at the back and was made of black beaver. The shape was very much like the French pattern of the same period, having a front which tilted forward. As with the first pattern Albert shako, there were 2 peaks, the one at the back fitting to the back of the head and continuing the line of the shako, the one at the front being horizontal and squared at the end. Above the peaks and encircling the shako was a leather band about $\frac{3}{4}$ in. wide sewn top and bottom. The top front of the head dress was decorated with a white over red worsted pom-pom which fitted into a gilt holder. A black leather chinstrap was fitted either side. The gilt shako plate was an 8-pointed star surmounted by a crown with the Garter belt and motto *Honi soit qui mal y pense* in the centre. Within the Garter on a black leather ground was the number 12 in gilt numerals. The other officer in the illustration is shown in the undress forage cap. This was made of blue cloth and was very floppy in appearance. The peak was of black patent leather and the cap had the number 12 on the front. The chinstrap was in black leather.

Uniform

The tunic was of scarlet cloth and double-breasted with yellow cloth collar cuffs and lapels. The collar was ornamented round the top and bottom with gold lace (field officer) and with the ranking at each side in embroidery. Lapels were made so that they could be worn buttoned over or turned back at the top to reveal the face colour of the regiment. Cuffs were round with a slashed panel in the face colour and were piped in white with the addition of 2 bands of lace on the cuff and 1 on the slashed panel. On the panel were 3 gold lace button loops and buttons. The left shoulder had a small scarlet twisted cord to hold the sash in position. There were 2 rows of buttons down the front, equally spaced with 9 in each row, the distance between the rows being 8 in. at the top and 4 in. at the waist. Buttons were gilt and bore the design of the number 12 surmounted by a crown, the whole within a wreath of laurels. Skirts at the back were piped in white with an inner edging of gold lace. On the panels were 3 regimental-pattern buttons. The top of the collar and leading edge was piped in white. The other officer is wearing the undress shell jacket in scarlet cloth with yellow collar and cuffs. Cuffs were pointed and decorated with 2 buttons, one on the yellow and one on the scarlet. Shoulders were decorated with twisted gold cords held with a regimental-pattern button. The jacket fastened down the front with small buttons equidistant. Trousers were in blue cloth with a scarlet welt down the outside seam of each leg.

Accoutrements

The officer in full dress wore a crimson net sash over the left shoulder with tassels hanging on the right side. The waist-belt was in white and fastened with a regimental pattern locket. There were 2 slings on the left side to hold the sword and 3 narrower slings to which the sabretache fastened. The sabretache was in black patent leather. The waist-belt in undress was of black leather with a similar gilt locket.

Weapon

Officers carried the regulation Infantry sword (91 A). The scabbard was all brass for field officers and brass-mounted leather for other officers.

3. 23rd Foot. Officer and Private, 1855

Head Dress

The second pattern Albert shako, as it was known, was authorised for use by the British Army on 16 January 1855. The body was made of black beaver for officers and black felt for the rank and file and measured $5\frac{1}{2}$ in. high in the front and $7\frac{1}{8}$ in. at the back, with the top tilted forward. The top was sunken and of black leather and measured 1 in. less in diameter than the bottom of the shako. There were 2 peaks, one at the front and one at the back. The back peak was a continuation of the shako and shaped to the head, while the front peak was horizontal and squared at the front. Above the peaks encircling the shako was a band of leather sewn top and bottom with a false buckle at the back. The top of the shako was adorned with a gilt

holder and a white ball tuft. A black leather chinstrap was fitted at each side. Field officers had the additional decoration of bands of gold lace around the top of the shako, the number depending on the rank of the wearer. The shako plate was gilt in the shape of a grenade and measured $4\frac{3}{4}$ in. from the tip of the flame to the bottom of the ball, which was ornamented with the Prince of Wales' feathers, a coronet and motto, in silver plate.

Uniform

The tunic was of scarlet cloth and was the double-breasted pattern adopted in 1855. Collar, cuffs and lapels were in the facing colour of the regiment, which in the case of the 23rd was blue. The collar had rounded corners and was edged in gold lace and decorated with the rank of the wearer. Lapels were made so that they could be worn buttoned over or turned back to reveal the blue lining. Cuffs were round, with a slashed panel in the same colour decorated with 3 buttons and gold lace button loops. The cuff and panel were edged in white. A cord of twisted scarlet worsted was fitted to the left shoulder of the tunic and held by a small regimental-pattern button. There were 2 rows of 9 equally-spaced buttons, the distance between the rows being 8 in. at the top and 4 in. at the waist. Skirts at the back were ornamented with 3 buttons and gold lace loops. The design of the button was a crown surmounting the Prince of Wales' feathers with the motto *Ich Dien*, the whole within a beaded circle. The leading edge of the tunic was piped in white. The private's tunic was in red cloth of the same design as that worn by officers but without gold lace. Button loops were of white tape. Trousers were of blue cloth with a scarlet welt down the outside seam for officers and a red welt for the rank and file. The officer's tunic was ornamented at the back with the flash fitted to the collar. The flash was also worn by Warrant Officers and Staff Sergeants until 2 June 1901, when this distinction was extended to all ranks.

Accoutrements

Officers wore a crimson sash over the left shoulder which knotted on the right hip. A white leather waist-belt was worn with 2 sword slings on the left side. The belt fastened with a regimental-pattern locket. The private's equipment was of the improved pattern introduced in 1850. It consisted of a white buff crossbelt worn over the left shoulder, suspending the black leather ammunition box on the right hip. A waist-belt was worn with a bayonet frog on the left hip. The leather-and-canvas pack or knapsack was worn on the back, with shoulder straps passing under the arms and over the shoulders. The mess-tin in oilskin cover and the blanket were fitted to the knapsack. In full marching order a water-bottle and haversack were carried.

Weapons

Officers carried the standard pattern Infantry sword (91 A) in a black leather gilt-mounted scabbard. Other ranks were armed with the Enfield rifle (94 A) with triangular bayonet (94 d).

Historical Note

The flash was worn from 1808. In 1834 Major-General Sir Thomas McMahon while inspecting the Depot Companies at Portsmouth ordered its discontinuance as a 'superfluous decoration'. The Commanding Officer was informed immediately, and he wrote forthwith to Lord Hill the Commander-in-Chief. On 28 November the Adjutant-General wrote to the Commanding Officer stating that the King had been graciously pleased to approve the flash now worn by the officers of the 23rd.

4. 93rd Foot Highlanders. Officer and NCO, 1857

Head Dress

The head dress worn while the regiment was engaged in quelling the Indian Mutiny or Bengal Mutiny was the home service pattern of feather bonnet. This is borne out by references in contemporary sketches and accounts. The head dress and indeed the uniforms of troops engaged in quelling the Mutiny were many and various, and no hard-and-fast statement of wear can be given, each regiment differing in its form of dress according to terrain, climate and supply. Various differences of dress during this period are excellently dealt with by D. S. V. Fosten in *Tradition* magazine. The 93rd wore the bonnet, in some instances with a quilted sun shade, about 14 in. high and with 6 tails hanging on the right side. The headband was diced, the left side decorated with a black silk rosette with a regimental-pattern badge. The bottom edge, bound in silk, hung down at the back in 2 tails. The Regimental Record mentions the lining of the head dress being removed. This gave better ventilation and made it lighter.

Uniform

The tunic was made of khaki holland cloth with red collar and cuffs. The collar was rounded at the front, and the cuffs were round with a slashed panel in khaki holland cloth. The panel was decorated with 3 brass regimental-pattern buttons. The shoulder straps were in red cloth. The tunic had rounded and cut-away corners to the front skirts. The kilt was in the Sutherland tartan. The officer's tunic was of the same design but made in alpaca, with scarlet collar and cuffs. Red twisted cords were fitted to each shoulder to hold the crossbelt and sash in position. All ranks wore the hose and spats.

Accoutrements

Officers wore the crimson sash over the left shoulder, knotting at the right hip. The crossbelt in white buff was worn over the right shoulder with 2 slings on the left side to suspend the sword. The belt was fastened at the chest with a regimental-pattern plate. For the 93rd this was a gilt plate with the crown surmounting a circle surrounded by thistles with the title 'Sutherland Highlanders' in the circle. Within the circle was the number 93 and below the thistles was a scroll with the honour CAPE OF GOOD HOPE. Rank and file wore the improved pattern equipment introduced in 1850. This consisted of a waist-belt with brass locket holding a bayonet frog on the left hip and a white buff crossbelt over the left shoulder suspending a black ammunition box on the right hip. Another black ammunition box was fitted to the belt on the right front. A small white pouch for percussion caps was fitted to the crossbelt. A water-bottle and haversack were also carried, and a rolled blanket or greatcoat was slung over the right shoulder, the ends being tied on the left hip. When officers carried the greatcoat or blanket the other shoulder was used. The sporran was of the regulation regimental pattern of black hair with white tassels, the black leather top bound in brass and badged.

Weapons

The rank and file were armed with the Enfield rifle (94 A), the regiment having recently replaced the 1842-pattern musket with this weapon.

5. 95th Foot. Officer and Private, 1857

Head Dress

In India the forage cap, in blue cloth with white cover and neck flap or curtain, was worn for the most part. The peak was in black leather. During the Mutiny head dress varied frequently from regulation pattern to adapted versions and even native head dress.

Uniform

The shell jacket, scarlet cloth for officers and red for other ranks, had yellow collars and cuffs. For officers the collar was decorated with ranking in embroidery. The jacket fastened by means of 10 buttons of regimental pattern, which bore the design of the number 59 surmounted by a crown within a circle. Cuffs were pointed and measured about $3\frac{1}{2}$ in. from the point to the edge of the cuff. Shoulders were ornamented with gold twisted cords. Shoulder straps of other ranks were in the face colour of yellow. Officers' trousers were white, and those of other ranks were blue with a red welt on each leg. There was no hard-and-fast rule on uniform, although within the regiment most dressed alike.

Accoutrements

The officer's waist-belt was in white with 2 sword slings on the left side. The private wore a white buff crossbelt with black ammunition box and a waist-belt with frog for the bayonet. On the crossbelt was a small pouch in white for percussion caps. Equipment was the improved pattern adopted in 1850.

Weapons

Officers carried the Infantry sword of the period (91 A). Rank and file were armed with the Enfield rifle (94 A) and bayonet (94 d).

Historical Note

During the Indian Mutiny the 95th took a ram from the mutineers, adopted him as their mascot and named him Derby. After the Mutiny, Derby was awarded the Mutiny Medal, which his successors continued to wear.

6. 55th Foot. Officer and Private, 1859

Head Dress

The officer shown wore the second Albert shako introduced in January 1855. It measured $5\frac{1}{4}$ in. at the front and $7\frac{1}{8}$ in. at the back and, made of black beaver with a leather top, had a band around the shako above the peaks. There were 2 peaks, one at the back shaped to the head as a continuation of the shako, and one at the front horizontal and squared at the end. The top of the shako was ornamented with a white-over-red pompom in an ornamental gilt holder. The shako plate was a gilt star surmounted by a crown with a Garter belt and motto in the centre. Within the Garter belt was the regimental number 55. The chinstrap was in black leather. The private is shown wearing the undress forage cap of blue cloth with the regimental number in brass on the front. The cap was fitted with a black leather chinstrap.

Uniform

The tunic was in scarlet cloth for the officer, with the regimental facecolour of green for collar and cuffs. The collar was rounded at the front, with gold lace around the top edge. The wearer's ranking was sewn to the collar at each side. The tunic fastened by 8 regimental-pattern buttons and the top of the collar and the leading edge was piped in white. Cuffs were round with a slashed panel, both in green. Cuff and panel were piped in white, and the cuff had the addition of a band of gold lace. The panel had 3 button loops in gold lace and 3 regimental-pattern buttons. Buttons were gilt with the design of the Chinese dragon above the number 55 within a crowned wreath. The back of the tunic was ornamented with 2 slashed panels piped in white with 3 buttons. The other ranks' tunic was of the same design and made of red cloth. Collar, cuffs and shoulder straps were in the face colour. The collar, cuffs, leading edge and slashed panels were piped in white with white loops on the slashed panels. Trousers were blue, with a scarlet welt for officers and a red welt for other ranks.

Accoutrements

Officers wore a crimson sash over the left shoulder, held by a small scarlet twisted shoulder cord. The waist-belt was in white japanned leather with a gilt regimental-pattern locket. There were 2 sword slings on the left side. Other ranks' equipment was the improved 1850 pattern consisting of a crossbelt over the left shoulder suspending an ammunition box on the right hip. On the crossbelt was a small pouch to hold percussion caps. The waist-belt, suspending a bayonet frog on the left hip, and the crossbelt were in white leather. The knapsack was of black canvas and leather and worn on the back. A haversack and water-bottle were also carried.

Weapons

Officers carried regulation Infantry-pattern sword in a brass-mounted leather scabbard (91 A). Rank and file were armed with the Enfield rifle (94 A) and bayonet (94 d).

7. 31st Foot. Officer and Private, 1860

Head Dress

The second pattern Albert shako was introduced on 16 January 1855. The body was made in black beaver for officers and black felt for rank and file. The shako measured $5\frac{1}{4}$ in. at the front and $7\frac{1}{8}$ in. at the back. There were 2 peaks of patent leather, the front horizontal and the back following the line of the head. The helmet plate was an 8-pointed star surmounted by a crown, with in the centre a Garter with the motto *Honi soit qui mal y pense* and, within, the number 31. The top of the shako was decorated with a red-and-white pompom in an ornamental holder. The chinstrap was in black leather with a buckle for adjustment.

Uniform

The tunic was in scarlet cloth for officers and red for other ranks. Collar and cuffs were in buff cloth. The collar was edged around the top in white piping with a band of gold lace beneath. On the collar was the ranking. Cuffs were round and edged in white piping with a slashed panel in buff, also edged in white piping. The cuffs had a band of gold lace around, and 3 buttons and gold button loops on the slashed panel. The leading edge of the tunic was piped in white, fastening with 7 buttons of regimental pattern. Buttons bore the design of the number 31 within a crowned Garter carrying the title 'Huntingdonshire' with also a wreath of shamrocks, thistles and roses. Skirts at the back were decorated with 2 slashed panels piped in white with regimental-pattern buttons. Other ranks' tunics were piped around the collar, cuffs, shoulder straps and slashed panels in white with white tape button loops. Trousers were in blue cloth, with a scarlet welt on the outside seam for officers and a red welt for other ranks.

Accoutrements

Officers wore a crimson net sash over the left shoulder held in position by a scarlet shoulder cord on the tunic. The waist-belt was in white leather with a gilt regimental-pattern locket and 2 sword slings on the left side. Other ranks wore the 1850 equipment with a crossbelt and ammunition box and a waist-belt with bayonet frog. A haversack and water-bottle were also worn. The pack or knapsack was carried on the back.

Weapons

Officers carried the regulation sword (91 A), and other ranks were armed with the Enfield rifle (94 A) and bayonet (94 d).

8/9. 79th Foot. Officer, Private, Colour Sergeant and Piper, 1860

Head Dress

The head dress worn by officers and rank and file was the highland bonnet. This was cocked and feathered with ostrich feathers. There were 6 tails hanging on the right side, the skull being 14 in. deep. The headband was of diced cloth with a rosette in black silk and a regimental badge or button on the left side. A vulture feather in a socket, left side, behind the rosette was 8 in. long. The bonnet worn by other ranks was of similar design but different in quality. The bottom of the bonnet was bound in black silk tape, terminating at the back and hanging. The piper wore a glengarry of blue cloth, bound around the bottom edge with black silk tape, joining at the back and hanging. The badge of the regiment was the Sphinx superscribed EGYPT. This commemorated the services of the regiment in Egypt during 1801. The badge was authorised on 6 July 1802. The piper wore a cock's feather in the glengarry.

Uniform

The officer's doublet was of scarlet cloth with collar and cuffs of the regimental facing colour which for the 79th was green. The collar was rounded at the front. For all officers not of field rank the collar had a $\frac{1}{2}$-in. lace band around the top. Ranking was shown on the collar. For officers not of field rank this was: captain – crown and star; lieutenant – crown; and ensign – star. Field officers had additionally a band of ½-in. lace around the base, and the ranking was as follows: colonel – crown and star; lieutenant-colonel – crown; major – star. Cuffs were round with a slashed panel of the same colour as the cuff. The slashed panel was edged around in gold lace with 3 regimental-pattern buttons and gold lace button loops. The doublet fastened with 9 buttons of regimental pattern. The Inverness skirts were piped in white, as were the pocket flaps. Flaps were further decorated with 3 buttons and gold braid button loops. Field officers had the addition of a band of gold lace on the edge of the flaps. Shoulder straps were of gold double cord, held with a small button of regimental pattern. The doublet worn by the colour sergeant was a shade of scarlet with collar, cuffs and shoulder straps of green. The collar was edged around the top in white which continued down the leading edge. Shoulder straps were piped in white and bore the regimental number 79. There were 9 brass buttons of regimental pattern down the front. These were convex with the crown in the centre surmounting a Garter belt with the motto *Nemo me impune lacessit*. Within the Garter was the number 79. Below the Garter belt and on both sides was a spray of thistles. Left of the crown was the letter V and to the right the letter R. Around the top edge were the words 'Cameron Highlanders'. Skirts and flaps were piped in white, and flaps were decorated with 3 buttons and white tape button loops. Cuffs were round with a

slashed panel of the same colour. Panel and cuffs were piped in white, and the panel had 3 button loops and buttons. The colour sergeant's ranking at this time was a single chevron on the right arm with, above it, the Union flag flying on the staff and at the bottom of the staff crossed swords. The whole was surmounted by a crown. On the left arm was worn a 3-bar chevron. The private wore a red tunic similarly ornamented to that of the colour sergeant but without his ranking. Pipers of the 79th wore green doublets. The kilt worn was of the tartan of Cameron of Erracht. Spats were white, buttoning on the outside for all ranks and worn with red and green hose-tops and red garter flashes. The change from the normal red-and-white pattern happened about 1858. The 79th changed to red and green, while the 42nd and 92nd changed to red and black; the 92nd also adopting plain grey for ordinary parades.

Accoutrements

The officer wore a white buff shoulder belt 3 in. wide with 2 slings on the left side, one long and one short, on which hung the sword. The belt was fastened on the chest by a regimental-pattern belt plate. This was a gilt frosted plate with burnished edge on which was mounted the crown surmounting a wreath of thistles with the number LXXIX across the centre. A crimson sash carried over the left shoulder tied at the right hip. Around the waist was the dirk belt with regimental-pattern rectangular plate. The belt was dark blue cloth backed with leather and embroidered with thistles in gold wire. The sporran had an embossed gilt frame and top and was highly ornamented with thistles. In the centre was the number 79 in gilt. The rest of the sporran was grey goat-hair with 6 gold embroidered tassels. The colour sergeant and private wore the infantry-pattern equipment of the period. This consisted of a waist-belt with brass locket, with the bayonet frog left and on the right front a white buff pouch. Over the left shoulder was a white buff crossbelt suspending on the right hip the black leather ammunition pouch. A small pouch was fitted to the crossbelt to take percussion caps for the rifle. The sporran had a black leather top edged in white metal with the regimental badge in the centre. The hair was greyish black with 2 white tassels in black leather holders.

Weapons

The officer carried the regulation claymore with scarlet lining and fringe (90 A). He also carried the dirk and skean-dhu, both of which were of regimental pattern. Other ranks, other than sergeant, carried the Enfield rifle (94 A) with socket bayonet (94 d). Sergeants carried the short pattern rifle with sword bayonet (94 g). The piper carried a dirk and skean-dhu.

Historical Note

At this period there were no regulations as to wearing of medals, hence the various positions shown in the medals of the colour sergeant and private. The piper has the bagpipe adorned with a regimental pipe banner. These were richly embroidered and usually fringed in gold. The 79th, on 10 July 1873, by express command of Her Majesty Queen Victoria, were ordered in future to be styled the '79th Queen's Own Cameron Highlanders' and to change their face colour from green to blue. They were granted at the same time the special badge of the thistle ensigned with the Imperial Crown. This badge was stated as 'being the badge of Scotland as sanctioned by Queen Anne in 1707 on the confirmation of the Act of Union of the 2 kingdoms'.

10. 32nd Middlesex Rifle Volunteers. Privates, 1860

Head Dress

The helmet was of black leather with 2 peaks, one at the back and one at the front. The front peak was edged with a white metal strip. The top of the helmet was decorated with a cavalry-style cross piece in white metal and ornamentally shaped with a plume socket measuring 4 in. high in the centre. The plume socket carried black feathers drooping over the crown of the helmet and had a ball at the base. The chinchain, of white metal interlocking rings backed with leather, was attached on white-metal rosettes to each side of the helmet. The helmet plate was a Maltese Cross surmounted by a crown with in the centre on a raised circle the intertwined initials V.G., for Volunteer Guard.

Uniform

The tunic was of scarlet cloth ornamented on the front with 5 rows of black cord, each row terminating in a trefoil knot. The top of the collar and the bottom edge were piped in black. Piping continued down the leading edge of the tunic and around the bottom of the skirts. Shoulders were ornamented with black cord, intertwined and ending in a trefoil on the end of the shoulders. Cuffs were decorated around with black piping and ending in an Austrian knot on the front. The back skirts of the tunic were ornamented in black cord. The tunic fastened down the front with 5 white metal buttons. Trousers were of blue cloth and had a scarlet stripe running down the outside seam of each leg.

Accoutrements

The waist-belt was of black leather about $1\frac{1}{2}$ in. wide and fastened on the front with a white-metal locket of regimental pattern. A black leather pouch, for percussion caps, was worn on the right front and a black leather frog on the left side. A crossbelt was worn over the left shoulder which suspended a black leather ammunition box on the right hip.

Weapons

Most of the Volunteers at this period were equipped either at their own expense or by the Government with the Enfield rifle (94 A) and bayonet (94 d or g), some Volunteers using slightly different arms.

Historical Note

The 32nd Middlesex Rifle Volunteers, known as the Volunteer Guard or the 6-foot Guard, were raised in 1860 during the great Volunteer movement. By 1869 the regiment had ceased to exist.

11. 41st Middlesex (Enfield Lock) Rifle Volunteers. Officer and Private, 1860

Head Dress

The shako had a black felt body with a leather top and a patent leather band ran round the bottom. The peak was horizontal and squared at the front. The chinstrap was of black patent leather. The shako plate was a star surmounted by a crown, with the regimental device in the centre. The plate was in white metal for other ranks and silver for officers. The top of the shako was ornamented with a dark greenish black pom-pom in a decorative holder. The body of the officer's shako was of black beaver. In undress the pillbox forage cap was worn, that of the officer having a silver netted button on the top.

Uniform

The officer's uniform was in black cloth with red facings. The tunic collar was edged around top and bottom in black mohair braid and on the collar, each side, were badges of rank. The leading edge was piped with square black cord which continued round the bottom edge of the tunic. On each side of the breast were 5 loops of black cord with netted caps and drops, and fastening with black olivets. The back was ornamented with a line of cord each side, forming 3 eyes at the top, passing under a netted cap at the waist, below which it ended in an Austrian knot. Shoulder straps were 2 rows of black cord. Cuffs were ornamented with a knot, type and size depending on rank. Overalls were of black cloth with a black mohair braid stripe down the outside seam. This stripe had a central line of red. Other ranks wore a tunic of rifle green cloth with collar and cuffs of the same colour. The collar was piped around top and front in red, which continued down the leading edge and around the bottom of the tunic. On each cuff was a knot in red cord. Shoulder straps were green, edged in red, and trousers were green with a red welt down the outer seam of each leg. There were 8 buttons down the front.

Accoutrements

Officers wore black patent leather crossbelts ornamented on the front with a badge, chain and whistle in silver. On the back was a black patent leather pouch with the Royal Coat of Arms on the flap. The sword belt was of black patent leather with regimental-pattern locket and with 2 sword slings on the left side, one long and one short, to suspend the sword. Other ranks had a black leather waist-belt with a pouch and bayonet frog.

Weapons

Officers carried the regulation sword with a gilt hilt (91 A). Rank and file were armed with the Enfield rifle (94 A) and bayonet (94 g).

Historial Note

The regiment was raised in early 1860, its services being formally accepted on 11 July. Members were mainly employees of the Royal Small Arms Factory, Enfield Lock, so officers were allowed the privilege of gilt-hilted swords and the Royal Arms on the pouch flap.

12. 77th Foot. Private and Bandsman, 1862

Head Dress

The private in the illustration in undress wore the pillbox cap, and the bandsman in full dress wore the 1861–69 pattern shako. The undress cap was made of dark blue cloth with a blue pom-pom on the top. The regimental number was fitted to the front of the cap. The shako was authorised on 28 November 1860. It measured $4\frac{1}{2}$ in. at the front and $7\frac{3}{4}$ in. at the back. The bottom of the shako was bound in a band of black patent leather. The peak was in black patent leather and squared at the end. The chinstrap was in black patent leather. The top of the shako was decorated with a white-over-red pom-pom in a brass ornamental holder. The plate was a star surmounted by a crown with a Garter in the centre. Within the Garter was the regimental number.

Uniform

The shell jacket was in red cloth and cut to the waist. The collar, cuffs and shoulder straps were in yellow, the face colour of the 77th. The jacket fastened with 9 brass regimental-pattern buttons. Buttons were convex, with the design of the Prince of Wales' feathers above the number 77. This was flanked each side with laurel leaves, crossing at the bottom. Where the laurels crossed was a scroll with the battle honour PENINSULA. Trousers were dark blue with a red welt down the outside seam of each leg. The bandsman's tunic was white with collar, cuffs, shoulder straps and wings in the face colour. Cuffs were round with a slashed panel, both edged in white. The flap had 3 button loops and buttons of regimental pattern. The leading edge of the tunic was piped in red, as were the ends of the epaulettes. The back of the tunic was decorated with 2 slashed flaps with buttons on each. Trousers were blue with a red welt on the outside of each leg.

Accoutrements

In the order of dress shown, the private is wearing no equipment, but in marching order the crossbelt with ammunition box, the waist-belt with bayonet frog, the haversack, water-bottle and pack would be worn. The bandsman wore a waist-belt with a frog for the band sword on the left side. On the right front was a black leather pouch for music cards.

Weapons

Other ranks were armed with the Enfield rifle (94 A). The bandsman wore the sword introduced in about 1850. It had a brass hilt, cast in one piece consisting of a grip and cross guard, the grip being decorated in Gothic style and the cross-guard finials being trefoil. In the centre of the cross guard was a square cartouche bearing either the Royal Cipher for Line Regiments, or the bugle horn stringed for Rifle Regiments and Light Infantry. Guards Regiments bore their regimental device (not illustrated).

13. General Officer, 1865

Head Dress

The cocked hat worn was in black beaver with a gold loop and button on the right side. At each end of the hat were crimson and gold bullion tassels. The top of the hat carried a plume of white swan feathers with, under them, red feathers long enough to reach the ends of the white ones. Midway between the gold loops and the tassels on both ends was a band of $1\frac{3}{4}$-in. black braid of oak-leaf pattern.

Uniform

The tunic was in scarlet cloth with blue collar and cuffs. The collar was piped in white and edged top and bottom with a band of gold lace. On the collar each side were badges of rank. Cuffs were round and ornamented with a slashed panel in blue cloth. Cuffs and panels were piped in white, the panel having gold-lace edging and the cuffs having 2 rows of gold lace. The panel was further ornamented with 3 buttons and braid loops. Buttons bore the design of crossed sword and baton, surrounded by a laurel wreath. Skirts at the back were ornamented with 2 slashed panels piped in white and edged in gold lace with 3 buttons on each. The leading edge of the tunic was piped in white. Trousers were in dark blue cloth with a scarlet stripe down the outside seam.

Accoutrements

A crimson net sash was worn over the left shoulder with tassels hanging on the right hip. The waist-belt was in white leather and fastened with a gilt metal locket. The belt had 2 sword slings on the left side.

Weapon

The sword carried was the general officer's pattern (90 B).

Historical Note

The officer is shown wearing the K.C.B. Military. The initials K.C.B. stand for Knight Commander of the Most Honourable Order of the Bath. The military badge is in the form of a Maltese Cross in white enamel, each point being tipped with a small ball. In each angle of the cross is a lion. In the centre is a rose, thistle and shamrock device with a sceptre and 3 coronets, the whole within a belt in red enamel inscribed *Tria Juncta in Uno*, surrounded by a wreath of laurels in green enamel, with the motto *Ich Dien* on a blue enamelled scroll at the bottom. The neck badge

is worn from a crimson ribbon, the breast star is worn on the left side. The star is a large cross, with the design of a wreath, belt and coronets in the centre.

14. Royal Artillery. Gunner, 1865

Head Dress

The busby was of black sealskin and measured $7\frac{3}{4}$ in. in the front, 9 in. at the back and slightly tapered towards the top. A red cloth bag, set $1\frac{1}{2}$ in. into the top, hung down at the right to the bottom edge of the busby. A brass grenade with flame was fitted to the left side, the flame forming the holder for a white hair plume. The design on the ball of the grenade was the Royal Coat of Arms with, below, a scroll bearing the motto *Ubique*. Beneath this scroll was the gun above a further scroll inscribed *Quo fas et gloria ducunt*. The chinstrap was in black leather $\frac{5}{8}$ in. wide. The body of the busby was constructed of cane and fur-covered buckram. The lining was of black cotton.

Uniform

The tunic was of dark blue cloth with a red collar. The collar was bound all round in yellow worsted cord. The tunic fastened down the front by means of 8 buttons of regimental pattern. The design on the brass buttons was a crown surmounting 3 horizontal guns. Cuffs were ornamented with knots in yellow worsted cord. The leading edge of the tunic was piped in red and the back of the skirts had 2 panels piped in yellow cord with 3 buttons on each. Shoulder straps were blue piped in red with the regimental title. Trousers were of dark blue cloth, and a 1¾-in. red stripe ran down the outside seam of each leg.

Accoutrements

The waist-belt was of white buff leather 2 in. wide with a bayonet frog on the left side. The fastening was a rectangular plate ornamented with a Union wreath and a scroll beneath with the word *Ubique*. Inside the wreath was a Garter belt with motto *Honi soit qui mal y pense* surmounted by a crown. Within the belt was the Royal Coat of Arms. A white buff crossbelt was worn over the left shoulder suspending a black leather ammunition box on the right hip. On the flap of the pouch was a field-gun badge. The knapsack was carried on the back by straps passing over the shoulders and under the arms.

Weapons

The weapon carried was the Enfield Artillery carbine (not illustrated) and sword bayonet (94 g). In the case of garrison Artillery the scabbard was all steel and not steel-mounted leather.

15. 26th Foot. Sergeant and Private, 1866

Head Dress

The head dress authorised for wear on 28 November 1860 came into general use early in 1861. The body was covered in blue cloth and bound round the bottom edge with a band

of black patent leather. The height of the shako at the front was 4½ in. and 7¾ in. at the back. The top measured 6 in. by 5¾ in. The shako of other ranks was plain; those of officers had bands of lace around the top. The number of bands depended on rank, officers of junior rank having none. The lace was gold for the regular army and in some cases silver for Volunteers and Militia. In certain Volunteer units the bands were placed around the bottom of the shako. A black leather chinstrap was fitted either side with a buckle for adjustment. The peak was horizontal, squared at the end and made of black patent leather. At the top centre of the shako in an ornamental holder was a pom-pom or tuft. In the case of line regiments this was white over red (Flank companies and their distinctive pom-poms having been abolished in 1862). In the case of Light Infantry the pom-pom was replaced by a dark green falling hair plume. An exception to this was the 46th Foot, identified by an all-red pom-pom. The shako plate was in stamped brass, the design being a star plate surmounted by a crown with the Garter belt and motto in the centre. Within the Garter belt, on a dappled ground, the regimental number was pierced out. The private in the illustration is wearing the forage cap. This was the pillbox cap with the regimental number in brass on the front centre. The top had a worsted tuft. In the case of the 26th the cap had a diced band around the bottom. There appears to be no order authorising this, as on 15 January 1858 a letter from the

Deputy Adjutant-General's Office asked about written authority for the deviation from the established pattern. Lt.-Colonel Hemphill replied on 24 February 1858 from Bermuda :

'Sir – In acknowledging the receipt of a copy of your letter of the 15th ultimo, addressed to the Officer Commanding the Depot of the Regiment under my command, I have the honour to acquaint you, for the information of the General Commanding-in-Chief, that there is no written authority with the Regiment for any deviation from the established pattern Forage Cap for the Army being worn by the officers and men of the 26th Regiment; but the present Bandmaster (a man of the highest respectability) states that the officers and men wore the same pattern Forage Cap as they now do when he joined the "Cameronians" in the year 1827, and that there were men belonging to the Corps at that time, of 26 years' service and upwards, who had never worn any other kind of Cap; and I have no doubt the same pattern has been used by the Cameronians ever since they were raised in the year 1689, it being national, and denoting the origin of the Corps. There are no letters or general orders with the service companies of the Regiment of an older date than September 1843. Under these circumstances, I trust His Royal Highness the General Commanding-in-Chief may be pleased to sanction the continuance of a Cap, the pattern of which has been of such very long standing in the Regiment.'

The reply was received from the Adjutant General's Office, Horse Guards, dated 31 March 1858:

'Sir – With reference to your letter of the 24th ultimo, I have it in command to intimate to you that the General Commanding-in-Chief is pleased to sanction the continuance of the present pattern Forage Cap in the Regiment under your command.'

Uniform

The sergeant in the illustration wore the tunic adopted in 1856. It was of scarlet cloth and single-breasted. Collar and cuffs were of the face colour, which for the 26th was yellow. The collar was rounded at the front and edged round in white piping, which continued down the leading edge. Cuffs were round, with a slashed panel in yellow with 3 buttons and button loops of white tape. Buttons were brass with the design of the number 26 within a continuous wreath of leaves. (This design in pewter had been worn previously by the regiment from about 1800.) The back of the tunic skirts were ornamented with 2 slashed panels with button loops and buttons, with 2 buttons at the waist above the pleats. Shoulder straps were of the face colour piped in white. The cuff and slashed panel were also piped in white. There were 9 buttons down the front of the tunic. The private wears the undress fatigue jacket. This was of red cloth with yellow collar and cuffs. The jacket was cut short, terminating at the waist. Trousers were of dark blue serge with a red welt down the outside seam of each leg.

Accoutrements

All ranks wore the equipment authorised in 1850 with the addition of a small pouch for percussion caps on the ammunition-box crossbelt and another white pouch for ammunition at the right front. The sergeant wore a crimson sash over the right shoulder knotted on the left hip.

Weapons

The rifle carried was the pattern 1853 Enfield rifle (94 A) with socket bayonet (94 d); sergeants carried the short rifle with the sword bayonet (94 g).

16. 68th Foot. Officers and Sergeant, 1868

Head Dress

The head dress was the shako adopted in November 1860, coming into general use in 1861. The body of the shako was covered in blue cloth with a blue cloth top and a black leather band around the base above the peak. The shako measured $4\frac{1}{2}$ in. at the front and $7\frac{3}{4}$ in. at the back. The peak of black patent leather was horizontal and square at the end. The top of the shako was ornamented with a dark green falling plume. The front of the shako was decorated with a star plate in brass surmounted by a crown. In the centre was a Garter belt with the motto *Honi soit qui mal y pense*. Within the Garter belt was the regimental number. The chinstrap was in black leather. The officer's shako was similar in design, but the fittings and cloth were of a higher quality. Field officers had the additional decoration of a band or bands of lace around the top of the shako. The officer on the right in the illustration wore the forage cap. This was in dark blue cloth with a band of oakleaf pattern lace around it above the horizontal black leather peak. The top was decorated with a black covered button and black braid tracing. On the front was a bugle horn stringed with the regimental number.

Uniform

The officer's full-dress tunic was in scarlet cloth with dark green collar and cuffs. The collar was edged around the top in gold lace and bore the rank of the wearer. Cuffs were round with a slashed panel, both in green. The cuff and panel were piped in white, and the cuff had an additional band of gold lace below the piping. The panel had 3 gold lace button loops and regimental-pattern buttons. The back of the tunic skirts had a slashed panel piped in white with 3 buttons. The top of the collar and the leading edge were piped in white. Buttons were gilt and had the design of a stringed bugle horn with a crown above, the strings going into the base of the crown. Within the strings was the number 68. The sergeant's tunic was of the same design, but the collar and cuffs were piped in white only. Button loops on the cuffs were white, and the shoulder straps were green piped in white. The badge of rank was in gold lace. Trousers were blue with a scarlet welt down the outer seam. The officer on the right of the illustration wore the frock coat which was in blue cloth with a blue collar and cuffs. It was double-breasted with 2 rows of regimental-pattern buttons, 9 in each row. Cuffs were round with a $5\frac{1}{2}$-in. slashed panel adorned with 3 buttons. There were 2 slashed panels at the back with 2 buttons on each, with 2 further buttons at the waist. On the left shoulder was a scarlet cord to position the sash.

Accoutrements

Officers wore a crimson sash over the left shoulder, knotting on the right hip. Both officers illustrated wore white leather sword belts fastened with a regimental-pattern locket and with 2 sword slings on the left side. The sergeant wore the crossbelt in white leather with the small pouch on the front for percussion caps and the big black leather pouch on the right hip for the ammunition. A waist-belt fastened with a brass locket suspended the bayonet frog on the left hip. The sergeant wore a crimson sash over the right shoulder. The black canvas-and-leather knapsack was worn on the back by straps passing over the shoulders and under the arms. On the pack was carried the mess-tin in oilskin cover.

Weapons

Officers carried the regulation Infantry pattern sword in a brass-mounted leather scabbard (91 A). The sergeant carried the short Snider-Enfield rifle (94 B) and sword bayonet (94 g).

17. Royal Engineers.
Officer and Sapper, 1869

Head Dress

The busby, of fur on a cane and buckram body, measured $7\frac{3}{4}$ in. high in the front and 9 in. at the back and tapered to the top. A Garter blue cloth bag, inset $1\frac{1}{2}$ in., hung on the right side to the base of the busby. A grenade and flame plume holder was fitted to the left side and held a white hair plume. The design on the ball of the grenade was the Royal Coat of Arms with supporters and a scroll beneath bearing the motto *Ubique*. The chinstrap was in black patent leather.

Uniform

The tunic was scarlet with blue velvet collar and cuffs for officers and red cloth with blue cloth collar, cuffs and shoulder straps for rank and file. The officer's uniform is fully described in Plate 20. The other ranks' tunic collar was piped around top and bottom in yellow cord. Cuffs were also edged in yellow cord, ending in an ornamental knot at the point. Shoulder straps were blue edged in yellow cord and the front of the tunic fastened with buttons of corps pattern. The leading edge was piped in blue, as was the bottom of the skirt and the back of the skirts below the waist. At the back were 2 buttons above the 2 lines of piping on the pleats. Trousers were in blue cloth with a scarlet stripe down the outside seam of each leg.

Accoutrements

Sappers wore a white crossbelt over the left shoulder suspending a black ammunition box on the right hip. The waist-belt, fastening with a brass locket held the bayonet frog on the left side. On the back was the knapsack or pack, held by straps passing over the shoulders and under the arms.

Weapons

Sappers were armed at this period with the Lancaster carbine converted to breech loading by the Snider principle (94 B).

18. 18th Foot. Officer and Drummer, 1869

Head Dress

The 1869–78 shako was authorised for wear in the British Army on 1 June 1869. It was copied from the contemporary French pattern. The shako, made of blue cloth, had a flat square-cut peak of black patent leather and was decorated with a band of gold lace around the bottom, 2 rows around the top and a row up each side. On the private's shako this gold lace was replaced by red and black braid. The shako measured 4 in. high in the front and 6½ in. at the back, with the top measuring 6 in. by 5½ in. The chinchain was of gilt interlocking rings backed with leather for officers and brass rings for other ranks. A white-over-red pom-pom in an ornamental holder was fitted to the top of the shako. On the back was a small hook to which the chinchain could be fastened when not worn under the chin. The shako plate was a wreath of laurels surrounding a Garter belt with motto, *Honi soit qui mal y pense*. The laurel wreath was surmounted by a crown. In the centre of the Garter the regimental number 18 was pierced out.

Uniform

The officer's tunic was in scarlet cloth with blue collar and cuffs. The collar was edged around the top with gold lace and had the rank badge or badges of the wearer each side. The top of the collar and leading edge was piped in white cloth. Cuffs were pointed and edged around the top with gold lace with, above and beneath, a trace of Russia braid terminating in ornamental knots. The skirts were piped down the pleats with white cloth with 2 regimental pattern buttons above. Buttons were gilt and bore the design of a crown surmounting a harp over the number 18, the whole inside a continuous wreath of shamrocks. The drummer's tunic was in red cloth with ornamentation in drummer's tape, which was of regimental pattern. This tape had been abolished in 1836 for rank and file except drummers, who wore it officially up to 1866.

Accoutrements

The drummer wore a white buff leather sling over the right shoulder, with a ring on the front which hooked on to the hoop of the drum. The officer wore a gold lace sword belt with slings, and over the left shoulder the gold sash with crimson lines and crimson and gold fringe and tassels on the right hip.

Weapon

The officer carried the regulation pattern Infantry sword (91 A). Drummers wore the band sword. (See Plate 12.)

19. Royal Artillery. Officer, 1870

Head Dress

The head dress worn after the Crimean War until 1878 by the Royal Artillery was the busby. The fur was black sable, and the busby measured 7¾ in. in the front and 9 in. at the back. A scarlet cloth bag was set into the top, with the fly falling on the right side. A gilt grenade was fitted to the left side of the busby, with the flames forming a holder for a white hair plume. On the ball was the design of the Royal Coat of Arms with a scroll beneath with the motto *Ubique*. Beneath this was the gun, and lower down a further scroll bearing the words *Quo fas et gloria ducunt*. The chinstrap was in black leather.

Uniform

The tunic was in blue cloth with scarlet collar. The collar was edged top and bottom with gold lace for field officers. On each side of the collar was the badge or badges of rank. The tunic fastened with gilt buttons of regimental pattern. The design on them was the crown over 3 guns, one above the other. The leading edge and the bottom of the tunic was piped in scarlet, as was the back of the skirt. The shoulders were decorated with twisted gold cord loops held with a small button. Cuffs were ornamented with gold lace and tracing in gold Russia braid. Trousers were blue, and a gold lace stripe ran down the outside seam of the leg.

Accoutrements

Officers wore a gold-lace crossbelt with gilt fittings of a buckle slide and tip. The tip was a grenade with a wreath around it. The pouch flap, edged in gold lace, had the same embroidery as the device on the ball of the busby grenade. The waist-belt, also in gold lace, had a snake clasp. On the snake was the motto *Ubique*, with on each side in a panel a lion over the crown. There were 5 slings, 2 wider ones for the sword and 3 narrow ones for the sabretache. The sabretache had a similar design to the pouch and an edging in gold lace.

Weapon

Officers carried their own pattern of sword in a steel scabbard with the hilt dressed with a gold cord and acorn knot (90 f).

Historical Note

The officer is leaning on a 12-pounder field gun adopted in 1859. The gun was a breech loader on the Armstrong system. It was also rifled. However, in 1870 a committee had decided that the breech loader was no advantage and the R.A. reverted to muzzle-loading guns. Breech-loading artillery was not restored until 1885.

20. Royal Engineers. Officers, 1874

Head Dress

The head dress worn at this period by the officers of the Royal Engineers was a black lambskin busby, first adopted in 1873. The top was of blue cloth. The busby was encircled with gold cord lines which were plaited at the front. At the top front was a gold corded boss. A gilt brass chinchain was attached at each side by a small gilt rose. A white plume was fitted in the top centre with a gilt socket. No badge was worn on the front, unlike the Rifles, who had their badges fitted on and below the corded boss. The busby was replaced in 1878 by the blue cloth helmet. The officer in undress wore the forage cap. This head dress, introduced in 1852, was of blue cloth with a black band of oakleaf lace, which in Royal regiments was replaced by a scarlet cloth band and in the Engineers by a gold-lace band. In the Infantry the number or number and badge was worn on the front. The peak was square and horizontal and made of black lacquered leather. The chinstrap was of black leather. On the top of the cap was a gold netted button and small loops of gold Russia braid. The cap was superseded by a new pattern in 1881.

Uniform

A scarlet tunic with blue velvet collar and cuffs was worn. The leading edge of the tunic was also piped in blue. The collar was edged with 'round back' gold cord with ¾-in. lace all round under the cord for field officers. There were 7 buttons at the front and 2 at the waist at the back above the 2 pleats edged in blue. The bottom edge of the tunic was also piped in blue. Cuffs were pointed and ornamented according to rank. Badges of rank were displayed on the collar in silver embroidery. The decoration on the cuff was an Austrian knot with Russia braid tracing. The amount of the tracing indicated the seniority of the wearer. The shoulder knots were of treble-twisted round-back gold cord on scarlet cloth. The trousers were of blue cloth with a $1\frac{3}{4}$-in. lace stripe down the outside seam of each leg. The officer in undress wore the shell jacket. The jacket was of scarlet cloth with blue velvet collar and cuffs. The bottom of the jacket was edged all round in gold braid, as was the bottom of the collar. There were small eyes in the braid at the ends of the collar and the bottom front. A crow's-foot knot of Russia braid joined at the centre of the collar seam and the waist. The jacket fastened by hooks and eyes, and the leading edge had a row of gilt studs down the front. Cuffs were pointed, 5 in. deep and ornamented with gold-cord knots. On each shoulder were twisted cords held by a small button of corps pattern. These buttons were convex gilt brass with the crown surmounting a Garter belt. On the Garter belt was the title 'Royal Engineers' and within the Garter the Royal cipher. Trousers were of blue cloth with a 2-in.-wide scarlet stripe down the outside seam.

Accoutrements

The officer in full dress wore the crossbelt, pouch and sword belt with slings. The crossbelt worn over the left shoulder was of red Russia leather 2 in. wide with 3 lines of gold-wire embroidery, each outer line being straight and the central line wavy. The crossbelt had a gilt buckle, slide and tip with the letters 'R.E.' in the tip. The pouch was of black patent leather with the badge in gilt of the Royal Arms with a scroll below with the word *Ubique* in gilt. The sword belt was also of red Russia leather, $1\frac{1}{2}$ in. wide with 2 lines of gold-wire embroidery. The front short sling, 1 in. wide, fixed to a D ring on the belt, and the back one of the same width was movable. The belt was fastened by a gilt burnished plate with the corps device in silver.

Weapon

The officers carried the 1856 pattern Royal Engineers sword (90 D).

21. 4th Foot. Private and Bandsman, 1875

Head Dress

The 1869–78 pattern shako was authorised for use by the British Army on 1 June 1869. The body was made of blue cloth and had a square-cut peak in black leather. (The shako was in green cloth in Light Infantry Regiments.) For other ranks the shako was ornamented with bands of red and black braid around the top, base and down the sides. The shako was 4 in. high at the front, $6\frac{1}{2}$ in. high at the back, the top measuring 6 in. by $5\frac{1}{2}$ in. An all-red pom-pom in the case of Royal Regiments was worn on the top of the shako in an ornamental holder. The chinchain was of brass interlocking rings backed with leather and fitted to the shako on each side with rosettes. There was a small hook at the back top of the shako on to which the chinchain could be fastened when not required to be worn under the chin. The shako plate was a wreath of laurels surrounding a Garter belt and surmounted by a crown. On the Garter was the motto *Honi soit qui mal y pense* and within the Garter the regimental number pierced out of the brass background.

Uniform

The tunic was in scarlet cloth with blue collar and cuffs. Shoulder straps were in scarlet cloth with the number 4 in brass on each. The bandsman's epaulettes were also in scarlet, but with wings decorated with white tape. The leading edge of the tunic was piped in white, and the cuffs were decorated with white tape terminating in a trefoil knot at the point. Skirts were piped down the pleats in white with a button at the waist above each line of piping. The tunic fastened with 6 buttons. Trousers were in blue cloth with a scarlet welt down the outside seam of each leg. Black leggings, introduced in 1859, were worn.

Accoutrements

The equipment worn by the private was the 1868 pattern valise, consisting of a white leather waist-belt with bayonet frog. Attached to the belt at the front were 2 dividing braces which crossed at the back, fastening back under the arms to the front of the brace. The valise was worn on the buttocks, with the mess-tin in oilskin cover above. On the shoulders was the rolled greatcoat or blanket. A water-bottle and haver-sack were carried.

Weapons

The regiment was armed with the Martin-Henry rifle (94 C) and bayonet (94 d).

22. 24th Foot. Sergeant and Private, 1879

Head Dress

The white foreign-service helmet was made of cork covered in white cloth with 6 seams. It was authorised for all ranks on 1 June 1877, though it had previously been worn in India and at other stations. This pattern of helmet continued in use until re-placed, later by the Wolseley pat-tern. Peaks and sides were bound in white cloth, and there was a 1-in.-wide piece of cloth sewn around the headband above the peaks, this being covered by a pugree in certain sta-tions, such as Hong Kong, Bermuda, and Malta. The back peak measured 12 in. from the crown to the edge, and the front peak measured $10\frac{3}{4}$ in. A zinc button, covered in white cloth, was fitted to the helmet at the top. From contemporary photographs in the authors' collection it appears that

the plate worn by other ranks on the foreign-service helmet at this date was the 1869–78 type. This fact is also borne out by the finding of 1869–78 shako plates on the battlefield of Isandhlwana.

Uniform

The service-dress frock tunic was of scarlet cloth, the collar also being scarlet but ornamented with grass green collar patches adorned with a small brass sphinx. Cuffs had a half grass green pointed panel edged in white tape, terminating in a crow's-foot knot at the point. Shoulder straps were also of scarlet cloth edged in white tape and ornamented with the number 24 in white metal. The tunic fastened down the front by 7 buttons, all general-service pattern, the regimental-numbered button hav-ing been discontinued for other ranks in 1871. Skirts at the back were plain. Trousers were of dark blue serge with a scarlet welt running down the outside seams and in marching order worn with leggings. These leggings were of black leather and measured about 9 in. in height. A leather strap $\frac{3}{4}$ in. wide, sewn around the top, ended in a brass buckle. A leather thong passing through 4 eyelets and securing on the leather strap fastened the leggings.

Accoutrements

The equipment was the valise pattern with white waist-belt and divided braces. Pouches were now white, having been of black leather until about this date. The blanket roll was worn on the shoulders, with the valise resting on the buttocks. Under the straps of the blanket was carried the glengarry. It was of blue cloth bound around the bottom edge with black silk tape. The badge was in brass and of the design of a Garter belt surmounted by a crown. On the belt was inscribed the title '2nd Warwickshire'. Within the Garter was a sphinx over a tablet bearing the battle honour EGYPT, with the number 24 beneath. A water-bottle was carried on the right hip and a haversack on the left hip, both with their own shoulder straps.

Weapons

Privates carried the Martini-Henry rifle (94 C) and bayonet (94 d) and sergeants the sword bayonet (94 g) in place of the triangular bayonet.

Historical Note

On 22–23 January 1879 the 2nd Battalion 24th Foot (2nd Warwickshire) (later the South Wales Borderers and now the 1st Battalion Royal Regiment of Wales) gained the distinction of being the regiment to have won the most Victoria Crosses in one action: seven. This record was nearly equalled by the Lancashire Fusiliers, who made their landing at Gallipoli in 1915, and won six V.C.s 'before breakfast'. Members of the 24th Foot who won the V.C. at the defence of Rorke's Drift were: Lt. Gonville Bromhead, Cpl. William Allen, Pte. Frederick Hitch, Pte. Henry Hook, Pte. Robert Jones, Pte. William Jones and Pte. John Williams.

23. 29th Foot. Officer and Private, 1879

Head Dress

The head dress worn was the newly adopted blue cloth-covered helmet. The body was made of cork and had 2 seams in the cloth on each side. The officer's helmet had a pointed peak at the front edged in gilt brass with a squared-off rear peak edged in black leather. Around the helmet and above the peaks was a band of blue cloth, sewn top and bottom. The top of the helmet was ornamented with a cross piece with a rose decoration on the end of each arm. A spike was fitted into the centre of the cross piece. On the back arm of the cross piece was a small hook to which the chinchain could be fixed when worn up. Running from under the back arm of the cross piece to the bottom of the back peak of the helmet and turned under was a gilt convex bar $\frac{1}{4}$ in. wide. The chinchain was of interlocking rings backed with leather and velvet and fitted to the helmet on 2 rosettes on the headband at each side. The plate worn on the front was an 8-pointed star surmounted by a crown. On the rays of the star was a wreath of laurels surrounding the Garter belt with the motto *Honi soit qui mal y pense*. In the centre was a badge and number of regimental pattern. The other ranks' helmet was also of blue cloth, but with the peaks rounded and bound with leather. Fittings were similar, but of brass and not of the quality of those on the officer's helmet. The star plate was of matching design, but die-stamped in brass and with the regimental number in the centre.

Uniform

The officer's tunic was of scarlet cloth with collar and cuffs of the facing colour, which for the 29th was yellow. The collar was edged at the top and front with gold lace and a Russia braid edging at the base. Badges of rank were also displayed on each side of the collar. Cuffs were pointed and edged in gold lace, with tracing of Russia braid above and ornamental knots below. The leading edge of the tunic was piped in white from the collar to the bottom. There were 2 regimental-pattern buttons at the waist at the back above the pleats, which were also piped in white. Shoulders were decorated with gold shoulder cords retained with a small button of regimental pattern. The button was in gilt, with the design of the number 29 within a raised circle. The amount of gold braid and lace on the collar and cuffs indicated rank. The other ranks' tunic was of scarlet cloth with the collar and cuffs in yellow cloth. The collar was edged around the base in white tape, and cuffs were ornamented in white tape with a knot at the apex. The back of the tunic had 2 buttons at the waist, with 2 lines of white piping down the back seams. The officer's trousers were blue, with a scarlet welt down the outside seams of the legs. Other ranks' trousers were of the same design but of a lesser quality. Leather leggings were worn in marching order.

Accoutrements

Officers wore a crimson sash over the left shoulder which knotted on the right hip. A white japanned sword belt with 2 slings, one long and one short, carried the sword. The locket was of regimental pattern. Other ranks wore valise equipment with white as distinct from black pouches common to the rest of Infantry of the Line. On the introduction of the valise equipment the much-prized star was transferred from the ammunition box to the valise. Official authority for the wearing of the star was obtained in May 1838. The 29th were granted permission for white pouches by a Horse Guards letter of 7 August 1877 which stated: 'I am directed by H.R.H. the Field Marshal Commanding-in-Chief to acquaint you that as the Stars that were recently ordered to be removed from the pouches of the 29th Regiment were granted to that Corps as a special distinction for service in the field, His Royal Highness, with a view to the assimilation as much as possible of the pouches of the 29th Regiment to those of the Guards has approved of white ammunition pouches being issued instead of black ones.' A haversack was worn on the left hip and water-bottle on the right hip from straps over the shoulders.

Weapons

The 29th were armed with the Martini-Henry rifle (94 C) and triangular bayonet (94 d), sergeants having a sword bayonet (94 g). Officers carried the standard pattern infantry officer's sword (91 A).

24/25. 24th Foot. Colour Party, 1880

Head Dress

The head dress was the regulation Home pattern cork helmet usually referred to as the blue cloth helmet, introduced by General Order 40 of May 1878. It had been on trial with a few regiments since 1876. The officer's helmet was of cork covered in blue cloth with 4 seams, 2 each side. Front and back peaks were also covered in blue cloth, but without any seams. The front pointed peak was bound with a gilt brass strip $\frac{3}{16}$ in. wide, and the back peak, square at the bottom, was bound in black patent leather $\frac{1}{8}$ in. wide. Above the peaks and circling the helmet was a cloth band $\frac{3}{4}$ in. wide sewn top and bottom. Measurements of the helmet were: back peak to centre of crown – $10\frac{1}{2}$ in.; front peak to centre of crown – $10\frac{1}{4}$ in.; side to centre of crown – 8 in. The chinchain was of gilt brass interlocking rings backed with a strip of leather and black velvet, attached to the helmet by means of gilt rosettes. A gilt brass convex bar $\frac{1}{4}$ in. wide ran down the centre back of the helmet, fastened by means of 2 brass studs, with a flattened continuation of the bar under the back peak. The top of the helmet was ornamented with a gilt spike and cross piece, the total height being $3\frac{1}{4}$ in. The cross piece was ornamented with 5 roses, 1 at the top into which the spike

screwed and 4 more at the end of each arm of the cross piece. A gilt hook protruded from the back arm of the cross piece to enable the wearer to attach the chinchain to it when not worn under the chin. The helmet plate was of the design of an 8-pointed star surmounted by a crown. In the centre, surrounded by an open wreath of laurels, was the Garter belt inscribed with the motto *Honi soit qui mal y pense*. Within the Garter belt was a sphinx over the word EGYPT and with the roman numerals XXIV underneath. Helmet plate dimensions were: top of crown to bottom of plate – 5 in.; extreme horizontal width of star – $4\frac{1}{4}$ in. The helmet for the rank and file was of the same basic design as that worn by officers but with rounded peaks, the front peak having a binding of leather instead of gilt brass. Helmet fittings were all made of stamped brass. The helmet plate was the universal pattern plate, die-stamped in brass with the design of a wreath of laurels surrounding a Garter belt bearing the motto *Honi soit qui mal y pense*, this being on an 8-pointed star surmounted by a crown. In the centre of the Garter belt was the number 24. The illustration, taken from a photograph in the authors' collection, shows colour sergeants and sergeant wearing the 1869–78-pattern shako plate, which was in the form of a wreath of laurels surmounted by a crown with the Garter belt and motto inside the wreath. Within the Garter belt was the number 24 pierced out of the dappled brass background. The 1869 shako and plate continued to be worn by depot companies until 1881.

Uniform

The officer's tunic was of scarlet cloth and grass green collar and cuffs, with 8 buttons down the front. Buttons of regimental pattern were convex gilt brass with a scalloped edge, having in the centre the number 24 surrounded by a wreath of laurels. The collar was ornamented with $\frac{5}{8}$-in. gold lace at the top and gold Russia braid at the bottom. The collar was further decorated with the badge of the sphinx on a tablet inscribed EGYPT and the wearer's rank behind this. Cuffs were pointed with $\frac{5}{8}$-in. gold lace around the top and a tracing of Russia braid above and below the lace, the lower terminating in a crow's-foot knot on the face colour and above in an Austrian knot. The leading edge and the top of the collar were piped in white. Skirts at the back of the tunic were plain except for 2 regimental-pattern buttons at the waist, with 2 vertical lines of white piping beneath reaching to the edge of the skirt. Shoulders were decorated with gold cords retained at the top by a small button. The field officer, on the left in the illustration, had additional rows of Russia braid in the form of small loops on the collar and 2 bars of lace on the cuff, showing $\frac{1}{4}$ in. of face cloth between the bars as well as additional Russia braid above and below the lace. Other ranks' tunics were also in scarlet cloth with grass green collar patches and cuffs. The collar was plain except for the sphinx collar

badge in brass. The bottom edge of the collar was piped all round in white, and this continued down the leading edge of the tunic. Cuffs were decorated with a half panel of grass green cloth edged in white tape with a crow's-foot knot at the top. The plain skirts had 2 buttons at the waist and 2 vertical lines of white piping from the buttons to the edge of the skirt. Other ranks' buttons were the regulation general-service pattern, the regimental pattern having been discontinued in 1871. Shoulder straps were in scarlet cloth edged in white tape and decorated with the number 24 in white metal. Trousers were of blue cloth with a $\frac{1}{4}$-in. scarlet welt down the outer seams of each leg. The only difference between the trousers of officers and rank and file was that of quality.

Accoutrements

The 3 officers in the illustration wore the regulation-pattern waist-belt of white buff leather with the regimental-pattern buckle or locket. The waist-belt was $1\frac{1}{2}$ in. wide and had 2 sword slings on the left side, one long and one short. On the top of the short sling was a brass hook on which the sword could be worn hooked up to the belt. The buckle was a round gilt clasp with the number 24 surmounted by a crown in the centre and a circle with the title '2nd Warwickshire Regiment' around the edge. Both halves had universal-pattern ends to attach to the belt. The centre interlocked with the outer part to form the buckle. The 2 lieutenants wore white buff leather Colour belts with gilt buckle, slide and tip and a gilt cup to take the bottom of the staff of the Colour. Officers wore crimson net sashes over the left shoulder, and colour sergeants wore crimson woven sashes over the right shoulder. On state occasions the officer's crimson sash was replaced by one of gold and crimson.

Weapons

Officers carried the regulation Infantry pattern sword in a steel scabbard, the hilt decorated with a white buff sword knot (91 A). Other ranks were armed with the Martini-Henry rifle (94 C) and bayonet (94 d).

Colours

The Colours shown in the illustration were presented to the 24th Regiment (2nd Warwickshire) (later South Wales Borderers and now 1st Battalion The Royal Regiment of Wales) on 21 June 1866 at the Curragh by the Countess of Kimberley, wife of the Lord Lieutenant. The Queen's Colour was lost at the battle of Isandhlwana on 22 January 1879, the Regimental Colour having been left at Helpmakaar. The Queen's Colour was subsequently found by Lieutenant-Colonel Black on 4 February 1879. In 1880 the regiment, having returned from South Africa and now stationed at Gosport, the Queen expressed a wish to see the rescued Colour. On 28 July 1880 Lieutenant-Colonel J. M. G. Tongue, with Lieutenants Phipps and Weallens and four colour sergeants, escorted the Colours to Osborne, where Queen Victoria attached a wreath of Immortelles to the staff of the Queen's Colour. A letter from the War Office dated 15 December 1880 stated: 'Her Majesty has been graciously pleased to command that a silver wreath shall in future be borne round the staff of the Queen's Colour of the 24th Regiment.' The Colours shown were borne by the 1st Battalion until 28 March 1933 when, on the Race Course at Hong Kong, the Governor Sir William Peel presented new ones to the Battalion. The Colours shown in the illustration were in accordance with the Queen's Regulations and Orders for the Army 1859. They measured 4 ft. flying and 3 ft. 6 in. deep. It would also appear that they were altered in accordance with the regulations of 1868 and 1873. In 1868 the pike was surmounted by a gilt brass Royal Crest instead of the spear head. In 1873 the length of the staff was reduced from 9 ft. 10 in. to 8 ft. 7½ in. Until their laying up in 1933 honours were added when authorised, those for the First World War being on the Queen's Colour and not on the Regimental Colour. The Queen's Colour was the Union, with the crown and regimental number in the centre on the cross of St George. The fringe was gold and crimson. The Regimental Colour was grass green with a small Union flag at the top nearest the staff.

In the centre was the crown surmounting a circle with the title 2nd Warwickshire and within it the number XXIV. On either side of the circle was a Union wreath of roses, thistles and shamrocks. On either side of the wreath and ranged one above the other were the battle honours. On the left from top to bottom they were: CAPE OF GOOD HOPE 1806, FUENTES D'ONOR, VITTORIA, NIVELLE PENINSULA, CHILLIANWALLAH. On the right from top to bottom they were: TALAVERA, SALAMANCA, PYRENEES, ORTHEZ, PUNJAUB and GOOJERAT. Under the Union wreath was the scroll with the honour EGYPT above the Sphinx, with a small spray of foliage below. The cords were gold and green.

Historical Note

As already stated, our illustration is taken from a photograph in the authors' collection. This depicts the Colours and Colour party after they had been presented to the Queen at Osborne. The officer on the left is Lieutenant-Colonel J. M. G. Tongue, who was commissioned into the regiment with the rank of Ensign on 24 February 1857. His career was as follows: Lieutenant – 16 April 1858; Captain – 29 August 1866; Major – 23 January 1879; Lieutenant-Colonel – 29 November 1879; Colonel – 29 November 1883. He left the Regiment to command the School of Musketry at Hythe on 31 January 1885, and from there in 1891 to command troops in Barbados with the local rank of Major-General. He died in 1892. The other 2 officers are Lieutenants Phipps and Weallens, who together with Lieutenant-Colonel Tongue served in the Zulu War of 1879 and were all present at the battle of Ulundi, Lieutenant Phipps being severely wounded and mentioned in despatches.

26. Royal Artillery. Officers, 1881

Head Dress

The head dress worn by officers and other ranks of the Royal Artillery in 1881 was the blue cloth-covered helmet introduced by General Order in May 1878. The body of the helmet was covered in blue cloth with 2 seams each side. The back peak was squared off and bound in leather and the front peak pointed and bound in a gilt brass strip. Above the peaks and around the helmet was a band of blue cloth sewn top and bottom. On the top of the helmet was a gilt cross piece in which was fitted a gilt ball in a leaf cup. In 1878 the Royal Field and Garrison Artillery had adopted the helmet, but with the standard Infantry-pattern spike adorning the top, soon to be replaced with the ball top. The cross piece was ornamented on the ends with roses and had a hook on the back arm on which the chinchain was fitted when not worn under the chin. The chinchain was of gilt interlocking rings backed with leather, fitted to the helmet at each side on a gilt rosette. The helmet plate was in gilt brass and of the design of the Royal Arms with the gun below. Above the gun in a scroll was the word *Ubique* and below the gun on another scroll the words *Quo fas et gloria ducunt*. The plate measured $3\frac{7}{8}$ in. high and 3 in. across.

Uniform

The tunic was of blue cloth with scarlet collar. Collar and sleeves were laced according to the rank of the wearer. The collar was edged all round with gold cord, and the leading edge was piped in scarlet, as was the opening at the back of the tunic skirts. The skirt at the back had 2 blue cloth panels edged in gold cord with a tracing of Russia braid inside the cord. On each there were 3 buttons of regimental pattern of the crown over the gun. There were also 9 regimental buttons down the front. Shoulder boards were of gold cord with the rank of the officer displayed in silver. On each side of the collar was a grenade in silver embroidery. Breeches and overalls were of blue cloth with a $1\frac{3}{4}$-in. scarlet stripe down the outside seam.

Accoutrements

The crossbelt was of gold lace 2 in. wide, backed with blue morocco leather, and with the buckle, slide and ornamental tip in gilt. The pouch was of blue morocco leather covered with an embroidered cloth flap. Within the edge of lace were the Royal Arms above and a gun below with oak and laurel wreath. The motto *Ubique* showed above the gun and *Quo fas et gloria ducunt* beneath. The waist-belt was also of gold lace $1\frac{1}{2}$ in. wide with a gilt S hook fastening bearing the word *Ubique*. Attached to the left side were 2 slings for the sword, 1 long and 1 short. For mounted officers there were also 3 slings to hold the sabretache, which was of blue morocco leather faced in blue cloth and edged in gold lace repeating the embroidered design of the pouch.

Weapon

The sword carried by officers of the Royal Artillery was that authorised for Royal Horse Artillery (90 F).

27. Black Watch (Royal Highlanders) (42nd and 73rd). Privates, 1882

Head Dress

A cork helmet covered in white cloth with 6 seams was worn. The edge of the front and back peaks were also bound in white cloth. A zinc button covered in white cloth on the top of the helmet screwed into a brass collet. A white pugree was worn around the helmet above the peaks. The chin-chain was of brass interlocking rings backed with white leather. A red hackle on the left side of the helmet fitted into the pugree.

Uniform

A scarlet unlined serge frock tunic was worn, cut similarly to the doublet but without the Inverness skirts. The collar of blue cloth had white edging tape around the base only. The cuffs were gauntlet-shaped in scarlet and ornamented with brass buttons of the general-service pattern and white tape loops. The tunic fastened by means of 5 general-service buttons down the front. Pocket flaps on skirts were ornamented with brass buttons and white tape button loops. The back of the frock tunic was plain. The kilt was of the Black Watch tartan. White spats with red and white checked hose tops were worn, with red garter tabs on the outside of the leg. Shoulder straps on the tunic, scarlet piped white, bore the regimental title.

Accoutrements

The sporran was of white goat decorated with 5 black hair tassels. The top was of black leather edged in metal and ornamented with the badge of St Andrew and the cross in white metal. The equipment was the 1868 pattern valise. Belts were of white buff leather with brass fittings. Braces were divided and crossed at the back. The valise was worn low on the buttocks, with the mess-tin in oilskin cover and the rolled blanket above. The bayonet was carried in a frog on the left side. Over the left shoulder was the strap supporting the water-bottle of the Oliver pattern on the right hip, with the strap supporting the haversack on the left hip over the right shoulder.

Weapons

Rank and file of the Black Watch were armed with the Martini-Henry rifle (94 c) and socket bayonet (94 d); sergeants with a sword bayonet (94 g).

Historical Note

The 1st Battalion Black Watch arrived in Egypt in 1882 as part of the expedition against Arabi Pasha, and bore the brunt of the fighting at the battle of Tel el Kebir with the rest of the Highland Brigade.

28. 3rd Middlesex Rifle Volunteers. Privates, 1882

Head Dress

The head dress in full dress and marching order was the cork helmet introduced in 1878. For drill order the pillbox cap was worn. The cork helmet was covered in grey cloth with 2 seams at each side. At the back and front were peaks covered in grey cloth and bound round the bottom edge in leather. Above the peaks and encircling the helmet was a band of grey cloth sewn top and bottom. The top of the helmet was ornamented with a cross piece with a rose on each arm. Screwed into the cross piece was a spike. The arm at the back of the cross piece had a small hook on which the chinchain was fastened when worn up. The chinchain was of interlocking rings backed with black leather. The helmet plate was in the shape of a Maltese Cross surmounted by a crown. On the cross was a circle inscribed at the top 'Third Middlesex', and in the bottom half 'Rifle Volunteers'. Within the circle was a stringed bugle horn. All helmet fittings were in bronze for other ranks and silver for officers. The pillbox cap worn in undress was about $2\frac{5}{8}$ in. high and piped around the top and bottom edge with a welt of red with a red covered button on the top. A black leather chinstrap was fitted to the cap.

Uniform

The tunic was grey, with collar and cuffs of the same colour. The collar was piped around the top and front in red, which continued down the leading edge and around the bottom of the skirts. There were 7 buttons down the front. Shoulder straps were grey piped in red, with the number 3 above the letters 'Mx'. Cuffs were pointed and piped in red with a knot at the apex. At the back of the tunic were 2 buttons at the waist above 2 lines of piping. Trousers were also grey, with a red welt down the outer seam of each leg. In marching order leggings of grey canvas with a red stripe down the outside seam and black leather bottoms were worn. The greatcoat was rolled and carried slung across the left shoulder, with the ends strapped together on the right hip.

Accoutrements

Belt and frog were in brown leather, as were the pouches. The belt locket was in white metal. Over the left shoulder was a leather strap suspending a felt-covered water-bottle on the right hip. Over the right shoulder was a canvas strap suspending the white canvas haversack on the left hip.

Weapon

In the year 1882 the 3rd Middlesex Rifle Volunteers were issued with the Martini-Henry rifle (94 C), which the regimental history states had been long awaited. This replaced the Snider-Enfield rifle (94 B). The bayonet (94 d) was the socket type for rank and file and the sword bayonet for sergeants (94 g).

29. Royal Inniskilling Fusiliers (27th and 108th). R.S.M. and Drum Major, 1884

Head Dress

The Drum Major in the illustration wore a large fusilier cap, in shape and style more nearly like that of the officers than of rank and file. The chinchain, of interlocking brass rings which tapered from wide at the side to narrow at the chin, was backed with black leather. The fur of the cap was racoon. The front of the cap was fitted with the grenade badge, with on the ball the Castle of Inniskilling with colour flying. The R.S.M. shown wore the forage cap. This was made of blue cloth with straight sides and with a black patent leather peak at the front, ornamented with a $\frac{1}{2}$-in. band of gold wire embroidery around the edge. The headband was ornamented with a $1\frac{3}{4}$-in. band of oakleaf pattern black lace. The badge on the front, in gold embroidery, was a grenade with the Castle of Inniskilling in silver metal on the ball.

Uniform

The tunic was in scarlet cloth with blue collar and cuffs. The collar was edged in gold lace, ornamented with a small grenade at each side. The bottom edge of the collar was piped in white, which in the case of the Drum Major, illustrated in full dress, continued down the leading edge of the tunic. The shoulder straps were scarlet and bore a grenade badge above the regimental initials, the straps being edged white. The Drum Major wore wing epaulettes edged and decorated in gold lace. For the R.S.M. the cuffs were round and edged with a band of gold lace. Cuffs on the tunic of the Drum Major were pointed and edged round in gold cord, forming an ornamental knot at the points. The tunic fastened by means of 7 buttons down the front. The back of the R.S.M.'s tunic was plain, as it was the undress one, but that of the Drum Major had 2 buttons at the waist behind above the pleats, which were piped in white. Ranking was worn on the right sleeve, the R.S.M. having a crown and the Drum Major a drum above 4 up-pointing chevrons in gold lace. Trousers were in blue cloth, with a scarlet welt running down the outside seam of each leg.

Accoutrements

Both R.S.M. and Drum Major wore crimson sashes over the right shoulder, knotting on the left hip. The Drum Major's sash was the ordnance issue pattern rather than a regimentally purchased one, which was usually more elaborate, bearing the honours of the regiment. The sash worn was in blue cloth edged in gold lace and ornamented with the Crown with Royal cipher beneath. Below this was a white metal shield with 2 small silver-tipped drumsticks. Beneath the shield were 3 scrolls with the title 'Royal Inniskilling Fusiliers'. The waist-belts, in white buff leather with brass lockets, had 2 sword slings on the left side. The Drum Major carried a mace in ebony or malacca decorated with silver chains with the silver top ornamented with the regimental name and honours. On the top was the Castle of Inniskilling in silver. The Drum Major also wore gauntlet gloves.

Weapons

Both Drum Major and R.S.M. carried the Warrant Officer's version of the regulation Infantry sword in a brass-mounted leather scabbard (91 A).

Historical Note

The bass drum of the 1st Battalion of this period is in the authors' collection. The background is the pre-1881 face colour of buff. At the top is a scroll with the title 'Royal Inniskilling', with below the designation '1st Battn.', followed by a scroll with the word 'Fusiliers'. Beneath this is the Royal Coat of Arms, under which is the honour PENINSULA. Then comes a wreath of shamrock decorated with enscrolled honours, and in the centre of the wreath is the Castle of Inniskilling above the sphinx and EGYPT. At the very bottom is the white horse of Hanover with the motto beneath on a scroll *Nec aspera terrent*.

30. Princess Louise's (Argyll and Sutherland Highlanders) (91st and 93rd). Officers, 1885

Head Dress

The head dress was the regulation pattern highland bonnet of ostrich feathers on a wire frame, in all about 11 in. in height and ornamented at the headband with a diced border.

The bottom of the head dress was bound in black silk with 2 hanging tails. A white vulture-feather plume was worn on the left side in a socket behind a black silk rosette ornamented with the regimental badge. Six ostrich-feather tails hung on the right side. The silver badge consisted of a wreath of thistles with a circle within bearing the title 'Argyll and Sutherland'. Inside this circle was the double cipher of H.R.H. the Princess Louise, with a boar's head on the left and a cat on the right. Above the cipher and on the circle was the coronet of the Princess.

Uniform

The doublet was of scarlet cloth with yellow collar and cuffs. The collar was edged all round in gold thistle-pattern lace with a trace of Russia braid beneath. The collar was further decorated with a badge in frosted silver of the design of a myrtle wreath intertwined with a wreath of butcher's broom. Within the myrtle wreath, in gilt metal, was a boar's head above a scroll inscribed *Ne obliviscaris*. Within the wreath of butcher's broom was a cat above a scroll inscribed *Sans peur*. Above the boar's head and cat was a label of 3 points. Cuffs were of the gauntlet pattern, 4 in. deep in front and 6 in. at back, edged around the top and down the back seam with gold lace. Cuffs were ornamented with 3 buttons and button loops in gold braid. The doublet fastened at the front by means of 8 buttons of regimental pattern. Buttons were of gilt metal and bore the same design as the

collar badge but surmounted by a crown. The Inverness skirts were $6\frac{1}{2}$ in. deep with a flap 6 in. deep ornamented with 3 button loops and buttons. The back of the skirt was ornamented in the same manner. At the waist at the back were sewn 2 buttons of regimental pattern. Collar, leading edge and skirt flaps were piped in white cloth. Shoulder straps were of gold twisted cord lined with scarlet, sewn to the doublet at the shoulder and held by a small button at the neck. The kilt was of Sutherland tartan. Hose were of regimental pattern, worn with gaiters of white canvas in review order and without in levee dress but with the addition of buckled shoes. A plaid was worn on the left shoulder fixed by a plaid brooch of regimental pattern which was not to exceed $3\frac{7}{8}$ in. in diameter.

Accoutrements

The waist-belt was of gold thistle pattern lace backed with leather and with a rectangular buckle of regimental pattern. A crimson sash was worn over the left shoulder with tassels on the right-hand side, and a white buff leather shoulder belt was worn over the right shoulder with slings 1 in. wide hanging on the left side to suspend the sword. The sporran in full dress consisted of a badger-head top and badger-fur body ornamented with 6 tassels. In levee dress the sporran had a gilt frame top backed with black leather and ornamented with the coronet, cipher cat and boar head. The body was of white goat's fur with 5 tassels down the front.

Weapon

Officers carried the claymore in a steel scabbard (90 A).

31. 1st Volunteer Battalion Royal Sussex Regiment. Sergeant and Corporal, 1886

Head Dress

The head dress was the blue-cloth-covered cork helmet adopted in 1878. It had 4 seams, 2 at each side. The front and back peaks were rounded, covered in blue cloth and edged in black leather. At the top of the helmet was a white metal spike and cross piece, ornamented at the end of each arm with a rose. The spike screwed into the cross piece. At the back of the cross piece was a small hook to which the chain fastened when worn up. The chinchain was of white metal interlocking rings backed with leather and fitted to each side of the helmet on white metal roses. The helmet plate was an 8-pointed star surmounted by a crown. On the rays of the plate was a wreath of laurels. In the centre was a circle inscribed around the edge with the regimental title '1st V.B. Royal Sussex'. A Maltese Cross was superimposed on a Roussillon plume with on the centre a wreath. Inside this was a Garter belt and motto, and in the Garter the cross of St George.

Uniform

The tunic was scarlet with blue collar and cuffs. The collar was rounded at the front, with a regimental-pattern collar badge at each side. The badge

was the same as that worn in the centre of the helmet plate, but smaller in size. The collar was piped around the bottom in white, this piping continuing down the leading edge of the tunic. Shoulder straps were scarlet and held by a small general-service pattern button in white metal. Shoulder straps showed the regimental title in white worsted embroidery. There were 7 white-metal general-service-pattern buttons down the front of the tunic. Cuffs were pointed and ornamented around the top edge, with white braid terminating in a knot at the point. The back skirt of the tunic was decorated with 2 lines of white piping from the 2 white-metal general-service buttons and reaching to the bottom edge of the tunic. Ranking stripes for non-commissioned officers were in white worsted tape. The long-service stars for volunteers as opposed to the equivalent stripes for the regulars were worn on the right arm and proficiency badges on the left arm. Trousers were of dark blue serge with a scarlet welt down the outside seam. In marching order black leather leggings were worn measuring about 9 in. high with a leather strap, $\frac{3}{4}$ in. wide, sewn around the top and terminating in a brass buckle and thong. They fastened at the outside with leather thongs, which passed through 4 eyelets.

Accoutrements

The equipment worn was the improved valise 1882 pattern. Straps and belt were of white buff leather, as were the pouches. Braces were divided at the front and shaped at the shoulders. A haversack on the left hip hung from a strap over the right shoulder. A strap over the left shoulder suspended a water-bottle at the right hip. In the illustration no valise is being worn. At the back at the waist was a rolled blanket, above which was the **D**-shaped mess-tin in black oilskin cover. The water-bottle was the Oliver pattern of 1875, which with a quart of water weighed 2 lb. 8 oz. It was made of wood bound with galvanised iron bands and was in the shape of a small barrel, but with a flat back to sit against the body. It was about 6¼ in. long and about 4 in. wide. There was a zinc stopper at the top with a wooden plug in the centre for drinking through. Most, if not all, of these water-bottles were made by Guglielminitti Brothers of Turin in Italy. Some were covered with khaki felt, but this was more usual in the cavalry version, which differed in having a tongue on the top iron band. The sergeant wore a crossbelt of white buff leather with white-metal lion head, chain and whistle. At the back, attached to the belt, was a black leather pouch ornamented with the regimental badge.

Weapons

All other ranks carried the Martini-Henry rifle (94 C) with socket bayonet (94 d), sergeants having a sword bayonet (94 g).

Historical Note

The regimental organisation at the time was normally 2 regular battalions numbered 1 and 2, with the Militia battalions numbered 3 and 4. After these there were the Volunteer battalions, which differed in number according to regiment. In the Royal Sussex Regiment there were 3 Volunteer battalions. The 1st was Brighton, the 2nd was Worthing and the 3rd was the Cinque Ports.

32. 1st West Yorkshire Volunteer Artillery. Officer and Gunner, 1887

Head Dress

The head dress was the 1878 pattern cork helmet covered in blue cloth. For officers the front peak was pointed and in Volunteer Artillery bound in silver. Helmet fittings were the cross piece and ball in leaf socket on the top, with a convex bar stretching from the top to the edge of the back peak, which was squared and bound in black leather. Other fittings were the 2 rosettes at the sides, to which fitted the chinchain of interlocking rings backed with leather and velvet. The helmet plate was in silver and of the same basic design as that worn by the Royal Artillery. This was the Royal Coat of Arms with the gun beneath. In the Volunteer Artillery the scroll above the gun and beneath bore either regimental titles or division titles. In most cases the top scroll was either blank, omitted or decorated with a laurel spray. The other ranks' helmet was also of blue-cloth-covered cork, with both the peaks rounded and bound in leather. Fittings and plate design were duplicated, but all were stamped in white metal.

Uniform

The tunic worn by officers was in blue cloth with a scarlet collar. The collar was edged in silver lace around the top, and for field officers around the bottom also. The collar was decorated with a grenade in gold embroidery. Leading edge and skirts were piped in scarlet and cuffs were ornamented with silver cord in a knot for junior officers and silver lace and Russia braid for officers of higher rank. Buttons were of the same design as the Royal Artillery, but in silver. The officer shown wore breeches of blue cloth with black boots. Breeches had a scarlet stripe down the outside seam. The gunner shown wore a blue tunic with scarlet collar. The collar was edged in scarlet cord and decorated with a grenade at each side. The leading edge and the back of the skirts were piped in scarlet. Cuffs were adorned with ornamental knots in scarlet cord, which in 1878 had replaced yellow cord for Volunteers for other ranks. Trousers were blue with a scarlet stripe down the outside seam.

Accoutrements

Officers wore the crossbelt and embroidered pouch. Lace on the crossbelt and embroidery on the pouch were in silver, but otherwise the same design as that worn by the Royal Artillery. On the pouch and sabretache the helmet plate design was repeated. Other ranks wore a white buff waist-belt with a black leather ammunition box on the right front. The flap of the box was ornamented with a white-metal field-gun badge. A water-bottle and haversack were carried.

Weapons

Officers carried the Royal Artillery sword in metal scabbard (90 F). Other ranks were armed with the Martini-Henry Artillery carbine and bayonet (not illustrated).

33. 1st Lanarkshire Rifle Volunteers. Officer and Sergeant, 1887

Head Dress

The head dress was the cork helmet of 1878. In the 1st Lanarkshire Rifle Volunteers this was covered in grey cloth. Peaks were bound in black leather around the bottom edge, and around the helmet above them was a band of grey cloth sewn top and bottom. The covering had 2 seams each side. The top was decorated with a cross piece with rose-ornamented ends, and a spike screwed into the centre. On the back of the cross piece was a hook on which the chinchain was fitted when not under the chin. The chinchain was of interlocking rings backed with leather, fitted to the helmet on rosettes. The helmet plate was Maltese Cross in shape surmounted by a crown. On the centre of the cross was a circle, with around the top half 'First Lanarkshire' and around the bottom half the initials 'R.V.C.' denoting Rifle Volunteer Corps. In the centre was a stringed bugle horn. All helmet fittings were in bronze. The officer's undress forage cap was of grey cloth with a black leather peak. The head band was diced and had the badge on the top front. The cap was worn in undress and had a black leather chinstrap. The top was ornamented with a netted button and tracing in drab braid.

Uniform

The tunic for rank and file was in grey cloth, with blue collar, cuffs and shoulder straps. The collar was taped around the base in drab, as were the shoulder straps, which also bore the regimental title in embroidery. Cuffs were round and edged in drab cord with an ornamental knot, which differed for sergeants and rank and file. The tunic had 2 buttons at the waist behind, above the pleats on the skirt, which were piped. Trousers were also grey with a blue welt on the outside seam. The officer's undress patrol jacket was in drab, with collar and cuffs of the same colour. The collar was edged round the top in drab lace and down the front and around the skirts at the back and each side of the 2 vents at the back. The front was decorated with 4 double drop loops of ¼-in. flat gimp drab, with eyes in the centre of each loop. There were 4 netted olivets on the right front which fastened to 4 loops on the left front. On each sleeve was an Austrian knot in drab. Shoulder cords were of twisted drab gimp and bore badges of rank. Trousers were also of grey with a blue welt down the outer seams. Leggings were worn in marching order.

Accoutrements

The rank and file wore the standard Infantry equipment of the period in black leather. The officer wore a black leather sword belt under the patrol jacket, with 2 slings hanging on the left side to take the sword. Sergeants wore a black leather crossbelt and pouch. The crossbelt was adorned with a chain and whistle.

Weapons

Rank and file were equipped with the Martini-Henry rifle (94 C) and bayonet (94 d), and sergeants the sword bayonet (94 g). Officers carried the rifle-pattern sword (91 A) in steel with 91 C in the cartouche.

34. Royal Military College. Cadets, 1889

Head Dress

The helmet was the regulation line-regiment pattern in blue cloth with 2 seams each side. There were 2 peaks, one at the front and one at the back, covered in blue cloth. The front peak was pointed and bound with a gilt brass strip, while the back peak was square and bound in leather. Above the peaks and encircling the helmet was a band of blue cloth sewn top and bottom. The chinchain was of gilt rings backed with leather fitted to the helmet at each side on 2 brass rosettes. A gilt convex bar ¼ in. wide down the back of the helmet was fastened by 2 studs. The top of the helmet was decorated with a spike and cross piece decorated with rose ornaments. The helmet plate in gilt metal was a star surmounted by a crown. On the star was a wreath of laurels around a Garter belt with the motto *Nec aspera terrent* on a blue enamelled ground. In the centre on a red enamelled ground was the Royal cipher in gilt. The cadet in undress wore the regulation dark blue cap with straight sides and about $3\frac{1}{2}$ in. high. The peak was in patent leather with a 1-in. band of gold wire embroidery around the edge. The headband was decorated with a band of black oakleaf lace with the badge of the initials 'R.M.C.' on the front.

Uniform

The tunic was in scarlet cloth with collar and cuffs in blue cloth. The collar was ornamented with $\frac{5}{8}$-in. gold lace around the top and a tracing of Russia braid around the bottom. Cuffs were pointed and had a $\frac{5}{8}$-in. band of gold lace around the top edge, with a tracing of gold Russia braid $\frac{1}{4}$ in. above and below, the lower braid terminating in a crow's-foot and eye and the upper in an Austrian knot. The tunic fastened down the front with 8 buttons of college pattern. There were 2 buttons at the waist behind above 2 pleats piped in white. The top of the collar and leading edge were piped in white. Shoulder cords were of round twisted cord lined in scarlet and fixed to the shoulder with a small button. The undress jacket was in blue cloth about 28 in. deep from collar to edge of the skirt. The front was rounded, and collar, cuffs and side seams were edged all round in black mohair braid. Trousers were for both forms of dress, in blue cloth with a scarlet welt down the outer seam of each leg.

Accoutrements

The waist-belt was in white leather and fastened with a gilt brass buckle with the design of a laurel wreath encircling the Royal cipher. The cadet in full dress also wore a crimson sash over the left shoulder.

Weapon

The cadet in full dress wore the regulation sword (91 A). The Lee-Metford rifle was used during drill (95 A).

35. Royal Military Academy. Cadets, 1889

Head Dress

The body of the helmet was in cork covered in blue cloth with 4 seams, 2 each side. The pointed front peak was bound with brass strip, while the back peak was square and bound in leather. Above the peaks was a band of blue cloth encircling the helmet and sewn top and bottom. The helmet was decorated with brass fittings and chinchain. The top fittings were a cross piece and ball in a leaf cup. The chinchain was of interlocking brass rings backed with leather. At the back was a convex bar running from under the cross piece to the edge of the back peak and fitting under it. The helmet plate was the Royal Artillery pattern. The other cadet shown wore the forage or pillbox cap.

Uniform

The tunic was in blue cloth with a scarlet collar piped in yellow cord, the leading edge and bottom of the skirts piped in scarlet. Cuffs were blue and pointed, with around the top edge a yellow cord ending in an Austrian knot at the point. Shoulder straps bore the initials 'R.M.A.W.' Trousers were in blue cloth with a 2-in.-wide scarlet stripe down the outside seam of each leg. The cadet shown on the left of the illustration wore a blue tunic and blue cloth booted overalls with a 2-in. scarlet stripe down the outside seam.

Accoutrements

The waist-belt and bayonet frog were in white buff leather, as were sword belt and slings.

Weapons

The cadet on the left carried the Artillery pattern sword (90 F). The cadet on the right has the Martini-Metford Artillery carbine and 1888-pattern bayonet (95 e).

36. Royal Scots Fusiliers (21st). R.S.M. and Private, 1890

Head Dress

The forage cap for the R.S.M. was of blue cloth and measured 3 in. in height. A diced band encircled the bottom, and the peak was of black patent leather with a thin band of wire embroidery around the edge. A red worsted toorie was worn on the top. The badge fitted to the front was of a grenade design in gold embroidery with a silver metal thistle on the ball. The private wore the regulation fusilier cap, which measured about 9 in. high and was made of black sealskin. The chinchain was of interlocking brass rings backed with leather. On the front was a brass die-stamped grenade badge with the design of the Royal Coat of Arms on the ball of the grenade.

Uniform

The scarlet frock tunic had blue collar and gauntlet cuffs, the former edged in gold lace and decorated with an embroidered grenade with the thistle on the ball each side. The collar of the private's tunic was taped around the bottom in white tape only. Gauntlet cuffs were edged around the top and down the back seam in gold lace for the R.S.M. and white tape for the private. There were gold-braid button loops on the cuff for the R.S.M. and white tape for the private, both with 3 buttons on the loops. Shoulder straps were in scarlet cloth and bore a grenade and regimental title. The R.S.M.'s frock tunic had pocket flaps on both sides just below the waist, edged in white tape and decorated with gold-braid button loops and buttons. Both tunics fastened down the front with 6 buttons. Skirts at the back were plain. The R.S.M. wore a crimson sash over the right shoulder with tassels falling on the left hip. The trews were of Black Watch tartan.

Accoutrements

The R.S.M. wore a white buff leather sword belt with a brass locket and 2 slings on the left side. The private is shown with just the waist-belt, bayonet frog and 1 pouch of the Slade Wallace equipment.

Weapons

The R.S.M. carried the claymore in a steel scabbard, here shown with the cross hilt guard (90 A). Rank and file were armed with the Lee-Metford (95 A) and 1888-pattern bayonet (95 e).

Historical Note

In 1877 the title of the 21st Royal North British Fusiliers was changed to the 21st Royal Scots Fusiliers.

37. 1st London Rifle Volunteers (London Rifle Brigade). Privates, 1890

Head Dress

The head dress was the shako of rifle green cloth bound around the bottom with a wide band of black patent leather. The crown was also black patent leather. The cloth body of the shako was seamed at the sides and was the same dimensions as the shako worn by Infantry from 1869 to 1878: 4 in. at the front and $6\frac{1}{2}$ in. at the back, the crown measuring 6 in. deep and $5\frac{1}{2}$ in. across. The peak was horizontal and squared at the front and made of black patent leather. The chinstrap was also of black patent leather. On the back top of the shako a bronze ornament covered a ventilation hole. The shako plate was a blacked star plate with, in white metal in the centre, a wreath of leaves encircling a shield with the

Royal Arms. Below this another smaller shield bore the arms of the City of London. Behind the central design was a crossed sword and mace. At the top of the shako was a falling dark green feather plume.

Uniform

The tunic worn by privates of the regiment was of dark rifle green with collar and cuffs of the same colour. The collar was rounded and dipped at the front, edged all round in black braid, which continued down the leading edge of the front of the tunic. There were 7 buttons of regimental pattern in black down the front and a further 2 at the waist at the back above 2 lines of black piping on the skirts. Shoulder straps were green edged in black. Trousers were plain and of rifle green cloth. Black leather gaiters fastening on the outside were worn.

Accoutrements

The equipment was all in black leather. The waist-belt, with white-metal fittings including the snake fastening buckle, had 2 pouches, one either side at the front, with 2 divided braces attached to the belt behind the pouches. On the back was the pack with rolled blanket and mess-tin. Over the right shoulder a belt suspended a black haversack on the left side. A bayonet frog was fitted on the belt on the left side.

Weapons

The men were armed with the Martini-Henry rifle (94 C) and the 1886 pattern sword bayonet (94 h).

Historical Note

The regiment was formed in 1859 as the 1st City of London Volunteer Rifle Brigade, becoming the 5th City of London Battalion of the London Regiment in 1909.

38. 1st Battalion Grenadier Guards. Pioneers, 1891

Head Dress

The head dress was the regulation black bearskin cap and worn not only by the Grenadier Guards but also by the other 2 regiments of Foot Guards. It measured about 10 in. high and was of fur over a cane body. A white hair plume was fitted in a socket on the left side for the Grenadier Guards, the Coldstreams had a red plume in the right side and the Scots Guards had no plume. The chinchain was of tapering interlocking brass rings backed with leather.

Uniform

The tunic was in scarlet cloth with blue collar and cuffs. The collar was decorated at each side at the front with a white embroidered grenade. The top of the collar and the leading edge of the tunic was piped with a $\frac{1}{4}$-in. white cloth welt. Shoulder straps were in blue cloth, piped in white. On the end of each was a crown surmounting the Garter belt and motto with, in the centre, the Royal cipher reversed and interlaced. Tunic buttons were equally spaced down the front and bore the design of the Royal cipher reversed and interlaced surmounted by a crown and a grenade

below. Cuffs were round and about $3\frac{1}{2}$ in. deep and piped in white around the top. They were decorated with a slashed flap in blue edged all round in white tape and with 4 buttons and white tape button loops. There were 2 buttons at the waist above 2 slashed panels with white worsted button loops. Between the panels was a central line of white. Trousers were in blue serge with a scarlet welt down each outside seam. Pioneers wore on the right arm the badge of their trade, this being for Grenadier Guards a grenade above crossed axes in white embroidery. Black leather leggings fastened with a leather thong and strap and buckle at the top.

Accoutrements

The equipment worn by the pioneers was the 1888 pattern of Slade Wallace. This was worn minus the pouches as pioneers were not required to carry a rifle. A variety of tools was carried including axes, shovels, billhooks; small axes were worn on the belt. Other implements such as hammer-claws, augers, sockets, chisels, files and gunspikes were among the numerous articles carried.

Historical Note

The establishment of Pioneers per battalion allowed 1 sergeant and 10 pioneers. It has been the custom in the Army for pioneers to wear beards. At the time of the illustration pioneers were directed by Queen's Regulations to do so if able.

Weapon

Pioneers carried the 1856 pattern pioneer sword (90 E).

39. Royal Welch Fusiliers (23rd). R.S.M. and Private, 1891

Head Dress

The R.S.M.'s cap was of black racoon skin and measured about 9 in. high at the front. The chinchain was of gilt burnished interlocking rings backed with black velvet. This attached to small hooks on the sides of the cap. The grenade worn on the front of the cap was gilt brass and bore Prince of Wales' feathers in silver. The private's cap was roughly the same shape, but the fur was sealskin and the grenade was brass with the feathers die stamped. The chinchain was of brass interlocking rings backed with black leather.

Uniform

The tunic was of scarlet cloth, with the collar and cuffs of the regimental face colour, which was blue for the Royal Welch Fusiliers. The collar was ornamented with $\frac{5}{8}$-in.-wide gold lace along the top and gold Russia braid along the base. The collar was further decorated with a silver embroidered grenade. Cuffs were pointed and ornamented with $\frac{5}{8}$-in.-wide gold lace around the top edge. Officers' tunics had additional decoration in gold Russia braid and lace depending on rank. Badges of rank were worn on twisted gold shoulder boards.

There were 8 buttons down the front of regimental pattern and 2 at the waist behind, with a pleat at each side edged in white cloth. The skirt was closed at the back. Collar and leading edge of the tunic were piped in white cloth $\frac{1}{4}$ in. wide. Shoulder straps were blue edged in gold lace and had a small regimental-pattern button at the top. The button was gilt convex with Prince of Wales' feathers within the title 'Royal Welch Fusiliers'. The private's tunic was of scarlet cloth and had a plain round blue cuff. Trousers were of blue cloth, with a scarlet welt running down the outside seam of each leg. At the back of the neck on the tunic a black flash was worn by officers, warrant officers and staff sergeants. The tails of the flash were 9 in. long and of black silk, cut in swallow-tail fashion.

Accoutrements

A crimson net sash was worn over the left shoulder knotting on the right hip. Around the waist was a sword belt of white japanned leather with 2 slings, 1 long and 1 short, to suspend the sword. The locket on the front was of regimental pattern. The private wore the standard 1888 pattern Infantry equipment.

Weapon

The officer carried the standard pattern Infantry officer's sword in a steel scabbard (91 A).

Historical Note

In July 1808 the custom of tying the hair in a queue with black ribbon was discontinued by the Army. The Royal Welch Fusiliers were stationed in Nova Scotia at the time, so received the order much later. When they finally gave up the queue officers continued to tie the black ribbon on the back of the collar. In 1834 officers of the 23rd were given permission to wear the flash as a dress distinction. On 2 June 1900 at the instigation of Lord Wolseley permission to wear the flash was extended to all ranks of the regiment.

40/41. 3rd London Rifle Volunteers.
Officer and Privates, 1891

Head Dress

The head dress, in common with most Infantry and Rifles at this period, was the cloth-covered cork helmet introduced in 1878. For Rifles and Rifle Volunteers and Light Infantry the helmet was invariably covered in green cloth. There were 2 seams at each side, and peaks were rounded and bound with leather. Above the peaks was a band of green cloth sewn top and bottom. In certain regiments of Volunteers at this period contemporary photographs show that the front peaks were pointed. The top of the helmet was ornamented with a cross piece, with roses on the ends of each arm and a hook on the back arm for the chinchain when not worn under the chin. The cross piece had screwed in the centre a ball in an ornamental leaf holder. The chinchain was of interlocking rings backed with leather and fitted to the helmet on each side with a rosette. Fittings were in white metal, as was the 8-pointed star plate surmounted by a crown

which was worn on the front. On the rays of the star was a laurel wreath encircling a Garter belt and the regiment's title. In the centre was a stringed bugle horn. The officer's helmet was of similar shape, except for the front peak being pointed and bound in silver strip and the back peak being squared. Fittings were the same except of higher quality. Roses on the arms of the cross piece were separate and screwed on rather than being part of the stamping. Stretching from the cross piece at the top to the bottom of the back peak was a half-round bar of silver-plated metal. The plate was of similar design but of higher quality.

Uniform

The private's tunic shown was of scarlet cloth with a buff collar. The collar was rounded at the front and ornamented on each side with a grenade. There were 7 buttons down the front in white metal. Cuffs were ornamented with a knot in white cord. Shoulder straps were scarlet edged in white tape and with the abbreviated regimental title embroidered on them in white worsted. The back of the tunic was plain. Proficiency badges were worn on the left arm and long-service stars on the right. Breeches were of khaki bedford cord and worn with dark blue puttees. The officer's jacket was scarlet with buff collar shoulder straps and cuffs. Badges of rank showed on the shoulder straps. There were 2 vents on the skirt at the back and the tunic fastened by 5 regimental buttons. The tunic had a patch pocket on each breast, the flap fastening with a small button. Cuffs were 5 in. deep at the point and 2 in. at the back. Breeches and boots were worn. The officer shown is wearing brown leather gauntlet gloves.

Accoutrements

Other ranks wore a version of the Slade Wallace equipment. Belts and pouches were in white leather. The belt locket was in white metal. A haversack was worn on the left hip and a water-bottle carried on the right hip, each with its own straps passing over the shoulders. No valise is shown in the illustration, but a rolled blanket and mess-tin in an oilskin cover are strapped to the back of the waist-belt. The officer wore the Sam Browne belt with one shoulder brace and a sword frog. All buckles and fittings were in brass.

Weapons

The officer wore the regulation rifle pattern sword with steel hilt in leather scabbard (91 c). Other ranks were armed with the Martini-Henry rifle (94 C) and sword bayonet pattern 1887.

Historical Note

The men depicted are the machine-gun section with a Gatling Gun. The man on the right of the illustration has the spare hopper or magazine suitably marked with the word 'rear' to prevent its being placed on the gun the wrong way. The Gatling was tried by the British authorities at Shoeburyness in 1870 and adopted for service in 1871. It saw action in the Ashanti War of 1874, the Zulu War of 1879 and the Sudan campaign. It was not universally liked because it was liable to jam, the fault of the cartridge rather than the gun. The cartridge was of coiled brass with an iron base which the extractor tended to tear off, leaving the case in the breech and producing a jam (96 A).

**42. Royal Niger Hausas.
Privates, 1891**

Head Dress

A pillbox-type forage cap was worn, made of blue cloth and measuring about 3 in. high. The top was slightly sunk and was decorated with a blue stem and pom-pom.

Uniform

The tunic was of khaki cloth and fastened down the front with 5 buttons. Shoulder straps were plain and held to the tunic at the neck by small buttons. Trousers, also of khaki cloth, were in fact long shorts which ended at the top of the calf. Dark blue socks reached just under the bottom of the shorts.

Accoutrements

A brown leather waist-belt fastened at the front with a snake buckle. Two ammunition pouches, one on the left and one in the middle of the back, were worn on the belt. A bayonet was carried in a brown leather frog on the left side. A brown leather strap over the left shoulder attached to a water-bottle which hung on the right side.

153

A white canvas haversack was worn on the left side, held by a canvas strap passing over the right shoulder.

Weapons

The Hausas were armed with the Snider-Enfield rifle (94 B) and socket bayonet (94 d).

Historical Note

The Royal Niger Hausas were raised in 1887 as part of the protective force of the Royal Niger Company. Officers were all British, and non-commissioned officers were all English-speaking natives, although a few British sergeants were used, chiefly as instructors in gunnery. As well as Snider-Enfield rifles, they were supplied with 12- and 9-pounder field guns, Nordenfeldt quick-firing guns and Maxim machine-guns. The Royal Niger Hausas had headquarters at Lokoja on the Niger river.

43. 1st West India Regiment. Sergeant and Private, 1892

Head Dress

In full dress the head dress worn was in 2 separate pieces. In undress, rank and file wore a peakless red cap with a white cord and tassel fitted in the top. In full dress, this was retained with the addition of a white pugree tied around it. The band and Corps of Drums had a small motif in the material of the pugree, and the lace of the uniforms of the Corps of Drums was the universal pattern drummer's tape.

Uniform

The uniform adopted by the West India Regiment appears to date from about 1860. It follows closely the Zouave style copied from the uniform of the French North African Troops of that name. Americans during the Civil War had regiments of Zouave-dressed men on both sides. The shell jacket was in white cloth buttoning up the front with 20 ball brass buttons. At each side of the row of buttons, reaching from the neck to the edge of the shell jacket, was a line of yellow worsted tape. The sleeves of the shell jacket had white pointed cuffs edged round in yellow worsted tape. Ranking for non-commissioned officers was worn on the right sleeve, and any proficiency badges on the left sleeve above the cuff. The waistcoat worn over the shell jacket was of scarlet cloth and edged all round in yellow tape. It fastened at the neck and was worn open as shown. Each side of the front edging of yellow tape was a zigzag of yellow cord, starting at the neck with each point ending in a small loop. There were 9 points in all, each side. Trousers were of blue cloth cut full and slightly baggy, with a yellow welt on each leg. They ended just below the knee and were tucked in white socks. Short white canvas spats were worn buttoning on the outside.

Accoutrements

White buff equipment was worn with brass fittings. The belt locket was the universal pattern with the motto *Honi soit qui mal y pense* in a circle and the Royal crest in the centre. The rest of the equipment was as for the Infantry of the period.

Weapons

The rank and file were armed with the Lee-Metford rifle (95 A) and 1888-pattern sword bayonet (95 e). Officers carried the standard pattern Infantry officers sword (91 A).

Historical Note

The regiment was formed in 1795, being called into existence in the *London Gazette* of 2 May, and besides the battle honours DOMINICA, MARTINIQUE, GUADALOUPE and ASHANTI took part in many small wars and expeditions. The regiment, part of the British Army, was disbanded in 1926. Officers wore the same uniform as officers of Infantry of the Line but with a special pattern of gold lace on the tunics. The facing colour of the 1st was white and the 2nd yellow. The helmet plate was the universal star, with a special pattern wreath within which was the Garter belt and motto. Inside the Garter belt on a burnished ground were the letters 'W.I.R.'. The regiment's battle honours were placed on the large rays of the star.

44. 10th Battalion Royal Grenadiers. Sergeant and Staff Sergeant, 1892

Head Dress

The head dress for full dress was the bearskin cap. It was about 10 in. high and had a chinchain of interlocking brass rings backed with leather. On the left side in a leather socket was a red-over-white hackle. In undress as shown a pillbox cap similar to that worn by the Grenadier Guards was used. It was of blue cloth about $2\frac{5}{8}$ in. high with a $1\frac{3}{4}$-in. band of scarlet cloth around the base. The top was piped in scarlet around the edge and the headband edged in black leather. On the front above the scarlet band was the regimental badge.

Uniform

In full dress a scarlet tunic was worn with blue collar and cuffs. The collar was rounded at the front and piped around the bottom edge in white, which continued down the leading edge of the tunic. There were 7 buttons down the front of the tunic. The cuffs were pointed and edged in white tape with an ornamental knot at the apex. The shoulder straps were scarlet, fixed at one end with a small button, edged in white tape and with the regimental designation in white worsted on each. On the collar at each side was a collar badge. Skirts had 2 pleats piped in white with 2 buttons above at the waist. The undress tunic was a scarlet frock with blue collar and cuffs. There was white piping around the bottom edge of the collar and cuffs. On each breast was a pocket with flap held by a small button. The shoulder straps were as in full dress. On the collar each side was a 6-pointed star. Trousers were dark blue serge with a scarlet welt down the outer seam. Leggings worn in marching order were about 9 in. high and fastened with a strap at the top and a thong passing through 4 eyelets.

Accoutrements

In marching order or full dress the valise equipment was worn with white belt and divided white shoulder braces. Black pouches were worn. Over the left shoulder was a strap suspending the water-bottle on the right hip, and over the right shoulder was a strap suspending the haversack on the left hip. The valise was worn on the back resting on the buttocks, with the blanket and mess-tin above.

Weapons

The regiment was armed with the Lee-Metford rifle (95 A) and bayonet (95 e).

Historical Note

The regiment originated in March 1862 when formed as the 10th Battalion Volunteer Militia Rifles, Canada. In November 1862 it was re-titled the 10th Battalion Volunteer Militia (Infantry) Canada. On 10 April 1863 once again the title was altered, and it was now the 10th or Royal Regiment of Toronto Volunteers. On 5 August 1881 the regiment assumed the title of the 10th Battalion Royal Grenadiers, becoming in May 1900 the 10th Regiment Royal Grenadiers. Finally, in May 1920, they were titled the Royal Grenadiers. In December 1936 they were amalgamated with the Toronto Regiment to form the Royal Regiment of Toronto Grenadiers. In 1939 on 11 February they took the title that the regiment still bears: The Royal Regiment of Canada.

45. Princess of Wales' Own (Yorkshire Regiment) (19th). Privates, 1893

Head Dress

The head dress was the regulation blue cloth-covered cork helmet introduced in May 1878. The cloth covering had 2 seams each side, and the 2 rounded peaks were bound in leather around the edge. The helmet top was adorned with a cross piece and spike in brass, and the chinchain was of interlocking brass rings backed with leather and attached to the helmet by 2 rosettes. On the front was fitted the helmet plate of brass. This was an 8-pointed star surmounted by a crown, with on the rays a wreath of laurels. In the centre was a circle inscribed round the outer edge 'Yorkshire'. Inside this came the cipher of H.R.H. the Princess of Wales combined with the Danish Cross and surmounted by the coronet of the Princess. On the centre of the cross were the figures 1875. The badge was adopted in 1881 on the abolition of regimental numerals. The Princess, who was born in Denmark, hence the Danish Cross, presented new colours to the 1st Battalion in 1875.

Uniform

A scarlet frock tunic was worn in marching order and for service training and manoeuvres, etc. It had a white collar and cuffs and was single-breasted, fastening down the front with 7 general-service-pattern buttons. The frock, introduced in 1873, carried no piping down the front or on the skirts. Cuffs were round. There were 2 pocket flaps, one each side below the waist. Shoulder straps were of scarlet cloth bearing the regimental title. On the left shoulder was a red cloth flap, its purpose being to prevent rifle oil staining the tunic. The flap was sewn around the edge and had a cloth loop on the inside which slid over the shoulder strap. There were 3 button holes, one to take the small shoulder-strap button and the others for the top 2 tunic buttons. Trousers were of blue serge with a scarlet welt down the outside seam of each leg. Black leather leggings, about 9 in. high, had a ¾ in. strap around the top ending in a buckle. Down the sides were 4 eyelets through which passed a leather thong.

Accoutrements

The equipment was of the 1882 pattern.
Belts were in white buff leather, and the locket on the front was the brass universal pattern. The divided braces attached to the belt at the front and crossed at the back and buckled back on to the other brace. The valise was worn on the back by 2 straps attached to the braces. A water-bottle and haversack were carried slung on each hip from cross straps going over the shoulders.

Weapons

The regiment was armed with the Lee-Metford rifle (95 A) and 1888-pattern bayonet (95 e).

46. 7th Middlesex (London Scottish) Rifle Volunteers.
Drum Major, 1893

Head Dress

The glengarry was made of dark blue cloth, the bottom edge being bound in black silk tape with 2 tails hanging at the back. The left side was ornamented with black-and-white cock's feather fitted behind a black silk rosette. The badge on the silk rosette was a large silver thistle.

Uniform

The doublet was in hodden grey cloth and had blue collar and blue gauntlet pattern cuffs. The collar was edged round in drab tape and decorated with a thistle in white metal each side. Cuffs were edged around the top and down the back seam in drab tape and had the further adornment of 3 buttons and drab button loops. The Inverness skirts were edged in drab tape, and the flaps had 3 buttons and loops in blue. Shoulder boards for the Drum Major were in twisted drab and held by a small regimental-pattern button. The leading edge of the tunic was edged in blue and fastened with 5 buttons. The kilt was also in hodden grey of the normal pattern. Spats were in white and fastened with white buttons on the outside. The plaid was in hodden grey and fastened to the left shoulder with a large silver regimental plaid brooch. The brooch was round and bore the design of thistles and the Lion of Scotland. The other ranks' tunic was of the same design, but with shoulder straps on which was borne

157

the regimental designation. Hose were diced.

Accoutrements

The waist-belt was in brown leather and fastened with a regimental-pattern locket in white metal. The Drum Major's belt had 2 slings in brown leather on the left side from which the claymore was suspended. The Drum Major's sash was in blue cloth edged with silver lace and bore the design of the Lion of Scotland, a thistle, a drum and another thistle. There were 2 small ebony drumsticks, one at each edge. The sporran had a grey goat's hair body with a brown leather top with the thistle badge in the centre. Tassels of black hair hung on the front of the sporran. The mace was of malacca decorated with chains and with a large silver coronet on top. Other ranks wore the standard Infantry-pattern equipment in brown leather.

Weapons

The Drum Major carried the claymore in a steel-mounted black leather scabbard (90 A) and a dirk attached to the right of the belt. Other ranks were armed with the Lee-Metford rifle (95 A) and 1888-pattern bayonet (95 e).

Historical Note

The London Scottish were raised in 1859 during the great Volunteer movement, being given the title 15th Middlesex (London Scottish) Rifle Volunteers. In 1880 they became the 7th Middlesex (London Scottish) Rifle Volunteers. In 1908 they became the 14th (County of London) Battalion The London Regiment (London Scottish).

47. 13th Middlesex Volunteers Queen's Westminsters. Sergeant and Cyclist, 1893

Head Dress

The helmet worn by the Queen's Westminsters was the regulation cork helmet that came into use in 1878. The body was of cork covered in grey cloth with 4 seams, 2 each side. There was a small rounded peak at the front and another, larger and rounded, at the back, both bound with black leather. The chinchain was of bronze interlocking rings backed with leather and fastened to the helmet on bronze rosettes. The top of the helmet was ornamented with a bronze spike and cross piece, $3\frac{1}{4}$ in. high with a rose on each arm of the cross piece. The helmet plate was in the shape of a Maltese Cross surmounted by a crown with a circle superimposed in the centre. Around the outer edge of the circle was the regimental title, and within this was the portcullis badge. The cyclist wore the side cap in grey cloth with a bronze badge on the left side. This was a crown surmounting a circle, with around the edge 'Queen's (Westminster) Rifle Vols'. In the centre was the portcullis badge.

Uniform

The tunic was of grey cloth with scarlet collar and cuffs. Cuffs were pointed and piped in white cord with an ornamental knot at the point. The collar was also piped in white, as were the shoulder straps which bore

158

the regimental title. The tunic fastened with 8 buttons down the front. Skirts were piped in 2 lines, and above the piping were 2 buttons. Trousers were of grey cloth, with a scarlet welt running down the outside seam of each leg. Gaiters buttoning on the outside were made of canvas with leather bottoms. The cyclist wore grey breeches with a scarlet welt on the outer seam of the leg and blue stockings and grey highland-type spats.

Accoutrements

The men wore the standard Infantry equipment, but the sergeant shown is wearing on the waist-belt a bayonet frog together with the roll and mess-tin at the back. A haversack and water-bottle covered in felt were also worn. The cyclist wore a bandolier over the left shoulder and the haversack suspended and rolled on the left hip from a strap passing over the right shoulder. The bicycle had a blanket strapped to the handlebars and a bucket in leather for the rifle attached to the saddle pole and the cross piece of the main frame.

Weapons

The regiment was armed with the Martini-Henry rifle (94 C) and bayonet (94 g).

Historical Note

The colour sergeant's stripes were of scarlet cloth edged in white with a crown above with crossed swords and the portcullis badge on the chevrons. Stars on the right sleeve were equivalent to long-service stripes in the Regular Army.

48. Queen's Own Corps of Madras Sappers and Miners.
Havildar and Sapper, 1893

Head Dress

A khaki cloth pugree was worn stretched over a stiff former. Officers wore the universal-pattern khaki helmet, decorated on the front with a regimental-pattern badge.

Uniform

The tunic was of khaki cloth which had been prescribed for all ranks in April 1887. The cuffs were plain, and the tunic fastened down the front with 5 buttons. There were 2 pockets on the chest, 1 each side with a box pleat in the centre and fastened by a flap and small button. Shoulder straps were also khaki and fastened with a small brass button. Trousers were in the same khaki cloth as the tunic.

Accoutrements

In marching order the equipment was in brown leather. The waist-belt fastened with a brass locket and had an ammunition pouch on each side. The bayonet hung in a frog on the left hip. Attached to the belt at the front were 2 braces which passed over the shoulders, crossed at the back and fastened to the back of the belt. A haversack and water-bottle were also carried.

Weapons

Other ranks were armed with the Martini-Henry rifle (94 C) and bayonet (94 g), which had been issued in 1888, replacing the Snider-Enfield (94 B).

159

Historical Note

On 10 March 1876, during his tour of India, The Prince of Wales, later Edward VII, was made Honorary Colonel and the Regimental title changed from The Madras Sappers and Miners to the Queen's Own Corps of Madras Sappers and Miners. The Corps had been raised as the Madras Pioneers in 1780 and reorganised by General Order of 1820 to become the Corps of Sappers and Miners. This order was not carried out until 1831. In 1903 the Corps became the 2nd Queen's Own Sappers and Miners. The title changed slightly in 1911 to 2nd Queen Victoria's Own Sappers and Miners, and in 1923 to Queen Victoria's Own Madras Sappers and Miners. In 1946 they became Queen Victoria's Madras Group, Royal Indian Engineers.

49. 30th Punjab Infantry. Havildar-Major and Havildar, 1894

Head Dress

The lungi was made of dark blue cloth tied around the head a number of times. The lungi ended on the left side in a white fringe that hung down. The front of the head dress was ornamented with a regimental-pattern badge. The Havildar in khaki uniform had a khaki lungi.

Uniform

The tunic was in scarlet cloth with white collar and cuffs. Cuffs were round and plain. The tunic fastened down the front with 9 buttons. There were 2 buttons at the waist at the back above 2 lines of white piping on the pleats. Trousers were dark blue with a scarlet welt down the outside seam of each leg. The shoulder straps of the tunic were scarlet. Blue puttees were worn. The Havildar in the illustration wore a khaki blouse which fastened down the front with 5 buttons. Trousers were khaki, as were the puttees.

Accoutrements

The Havildar-Major wore a white buff leather belt with a regimental-pattern locket in brass. A crimson sash was worn over the right shoulder with tassels hanging on the left hip. The Havildar in marching order wore the equipment of the 1882 valise pattern. This was a waist-belt with 2 pouches and 2 divided braces. A water-bottle and haversack were also carried.

Weapons

The rank and file were armed with the Martini-Henry rifle (94 C) and bayonet (94 h).

Historical Note

The 30th were raised in 1857 as the 22nd Regiment of Punjab Infantry, and later became the 34th Regiment. After this they became the 30th Punjabis and later the 30th Punjab Infantry. In the reorganisation of 1922 they became the 1st Battalion 16th Punjab Regiment. In battalions of Native Infantry a Havildar-Major was regimentally appointed as the Drill Havildar-Major.

50. 3rd Battalion Grenadier Guards. Guardsmen, 1895

Head Dress

The guardsman in marching order wore the regulation bearskin cap which measured about 10 in. high and was constructed on a cane body. The chinchain was of tapered interlocking brass rings backed with leather. A white hair plume was fitted to the left side in a small socket. The guardsman in undress drill order wore the pillbox cap. The body was made of blue cloth with a scarlet welt around the top and a scarlet band about 1½ in. around the base. A brass grenade was fitted on the front. The bottom edge of the cap was bound in black leather and a black leather chinstrap fitted to each side.

Uniform

The tunic was in scarlet cloth with blue cloth collar, cuffs and shoulder straps. The top of the collar and leading edge of the tunic were piped in white cloth ¼ in. wide. Cuffs were round and piped in white with a slashed panel on each in blue cloth, also piped in white and ornamented with button loops and buttons. Shoulder straps were piped white and had the badge of the crowned Garter belt with the Royal cipher in the centre reversed and intertwined embroidered on them. Buttons down the front were equally spaced. Skirts were ornamented with slashed panels which were decorated with button loops and 2 buttons at the waist above. Trousers were of blue cloth with a scarlet welt down the outside seam of each leg. The drill jacket was in white cloth and had a round-cornered stand collar. The drill jacket was cut like a shell jacket and reached to the waist. Cuffs were plain, with a regimental-pattern button on each. The jacket fastened with 9 buttons down the front. Buttons were in brass and bore the design of the Royal cipher, reversed and intertwined with a crown above and grenade below. Twisted white worsted cords were fitted to the shoulders, held by a regimental-pattern button. On the left side bottom of the jacket was a small brass hook which located and kept the belt in position.

Accoutrements

The guardsman in drill order wore the waist-belt and bayonet frog only. The guardsman in marching order wore the full equipment. This was the valise pattern, with the divided braces and the valise worn on the back.

Weapons

The Grenadier Guards were armed with the Lee-Metford rifle (95 A) and bayonet (95 e).

51. Royal Malta Artillery. Officer and Gunner, 1895

Head Dress

The head dress was the white foreign-service helmet adopted in 1877. The body was made of cork covered in white cloth, the peaks also being covered in white cloth and bound round the edge. Above the 2 peaks was a band of white cloth which went round the helmet and was sewn top and bottom. The back peak measured 12 in. from crown to edge, and the front peak was 10¾ in. The helmet top was adorned with a gilt ball in a leaf cup mounted on a gilt dome. When the ball was not required to be worn a zinc button covered in white cloth took its place. Under the rim, at each side of the helmet, there were 2 hooks to which the chinchain fastened. When not worn under the chin the chain was hooked up on the right side to a small brass hook. The chinchain was of brass interlocking rings backed with white leather. The front of the helmet was ornamented with the regimental-pattern helmet plate. The design was of a wreath surmounted by a crown, inside which was a Garter belt inscribed Royal Malta Artillery with a Maltese Cross in the centre. Below the wreath was the gun.

Uniform

The tunic was of blue cloth with a scarlet collar. The collar was edged all round, top and bottom, in gold cord and further ornamented with a silver embroidered grenade 2¼ in. long at either end. The tunic was single-breasted and fastened with 9 buttons down the front. The buttons were of the pattern worn by the Royal Artillery, in gilt convex metal with the design of a crown over a gun. Cuffs had gold cord and braid ornamentation according to rank. The leading edge was piped in scarlet, as was the opening at the back of the

skirts. Each side of the opening was a slashed panel edged in gold cord with an inner tracing of Russia braid. Flaps were adorned with 3 buttons, and there were a further 2 at the waist. Each shoulder was decorated with a twisted-gold-cord shoulder board, on which was displayed the ranking in silver. Overalls were of blue cloth and had a scarlet stripe 1¾ in. wide down the outside seam of each leg. Other ranks wore the uniform of the Royal Garrison Artillery. The tunic was blue with a scarlet collar, and the edging was in yellow braid, as were the ornaments on the cuff.

Accoutrements

The shoulder belt for officers was of gold lace and worn over the left shoulder, 2 in. wide backed with blue morocco leather. The buckle slide and ornamental tip, of a wreath and grenade, were in gilt metal. The pouch was embroidered on the flap with a crown surmounting a wreath with a Garter belt inscribed Royal Malta Artillery. In the garter was a Maltese Cross in silver. Below the wreath in gilding metal was the sun. The waist-belt was of 1½-in. gold lace lined in blue morocco leather. The slings, 1 in. wide, were attached to rings on the belt at the left side. There were also 3 sabretache slings ¾ in. wide in gold lace backed with blue morocco leather. The belt buckle was in the form of 2 ovals, each oval mounted with the Royal crest and joined by a snake fastening inscribed Malta, instead of *Ubique*, the motto of the Royal Artillery. The other ranks' equipment was of white buff, being the same pattern as the Royal Artillery.

Weapons

Officers of the Royal Malta Artillery carried the standard Royal Artillery officer's sword (90 F).

52. Cameronians (Scottish Rifles) (26th and 90th). Officer and Private, 1896

Head Dress

The shako introduced for the Cameronians in 1892 was of rifle green cloth, $4\frac{1}{2}$ in. high in the front and $7\frac{3}{4}$ in. high at the back, with the top and bottom bound in black tape. Black worsted twisted caplines were worn above the peak and hooked up at the side on small thistle attachments. A black corded boss was fitted to the top front of the shako and ornamented with a mullet in bronze, below which was a stringed bugle horn also in bronze. A black horsehair upright plume was fitted into the top front of the shako behind the corded boss. The mullet was the Douglas mullet or star. The officer's shako was of the same design but of higher quality. Before 1892, and from the date of the designation of the 26th Foot as the Cameronians (Scottish Rifles) in 1881, the cloth-covered cork helmet was worn.

Uniform

The doublet was of rifle green cloth, with collar and cuffs of the same colour. The collar was taped in black around the base, the piping continuing down the leading edge. Cuffs were of the gauntlet pattern, taped around the top and down the back seam and decorated with 3 regimental-pattern buttons and black tape button loops. The button was black, with the design of a crown and stringed bugle horn. The doublet fastened down the front with 8 regimental-pattern buttons. Skirts were about 7 in. deep, with the flaps of the Inverness skirt about 6 in. deep and edged in black and further ornamented with regimental-pattern buttons and black tape loops. The trews were of Douglas tartan.

Accoutrements

The equipment was the 1888 Slade Wallace pattern, but in black leather instead of the white buff leather. Fittings were brass, but the universal locket was replaced by a snake fastening. In marching order the full equipment was worn with black leather leggings.

Weapons

The Cameronians were armed with the Lee-Metford rifle (95 A) with the 1888-pattern bayonet (95 e). Officers carried the rifle pattern sword but with the Douglas mullet and thistles in the cartouche in place of the stringed bugle horn (91 H).

Historical Note

The regiment was raised in 1689 and were stern Covenanters who joined the Earl of Angus to preserve the Presbyterian Church. They were designated a Rifle regiment in 1881 and after some 280 years' service were disbanded on 14 May 1968 about ½ mile from where they were originally raised.

53. New South Wales Field Artillery. Officer and Gunner, 1896

Head Dress

The helmet was of white-cloth-covered cork adopted in 1877. It was bound around the bottom edges in white and measured 12 in. from back peak to crown and 10¾ in. from front peak to crown. The top of the helmet was decorated with a gilt ball in a leaf cup mounted on a dome base also in gilt. Around the helmet was a pugree of blue cloth with red edging at the top. On the front of the helmet above the pugree was an oval of red edged in yellow and with a yellow cross in the centre. At each side of the head dress was a hook under the rim to which fitted the gilt interlocking ring chinchain.

Uniform

The tunic was of blue cloth with a scarlet collar. The collar was edged all round in gold cord and ornamented with a silver embroidered grenade at each side. The tunic was single-breasted with the leading edge piped in scarlet which continued around the bottom edge of the skirt. The skirt was square cut at the front and open at the back, with a blue cloth flap on each side edged in gold cord and Russia braid. The opening at the back was piped in scarlet. On each slashed flap were 3 regimental-pattern buttons. There were also 9 buttons down the front of the tunic and 2 at the waist behind. Shoulders were decorated with twisted-gold-cord boards, on which were sewn the badges of rank. The sleeves were ornamented with gold cord or lace and Russia braid according to the rank of the wearer. Buttons were gilt convex, with the design of a gun surmounted by a crown. Breeches were light brown and worn with black boots and spurs. Overalls, when worn, were the same colour cloth as the tunic, with a 1¾ in. scarlet stripe down the outside seams of the legs. The other ranks' uniform was a blue tunic with scarlet collar ornamented with a grenade and edged in yellow cord and with a yellow cord knot on each cuff. Breeches were brown and worn with dark blue puttees and boots.

Accoutrements

A gold lace pouch belt for officers was worn over the left shoulder. It was 2 in. wide and lined with blue morocco leather and with an ornamental gilt buckle, slide and grenade encircled with a wreath tip. The pouch was in black patent leather with the badge on the centre of the flap. The waist-belt was also of gold lace lined with blue morocco leather 1½ in. wide. There were 2 slings, one long and one short on the left side from which the sword was suspended. The belt was fastened with a rectangular plate bearing the badge in silver. Other ranks wore a white buff leather sword belt.

Weapon

Officers carried the standard Royal Artillery pattern sword (90 F).

54. Victoria Infantry Brigade. Officer and Private, 1896

Head Dress

The helmet was made of cork covered in khaki cloth in 6 seams. Above the peaks and going round the headband was a khaki pugree. The measurements of the helmet were: back peak to crown 12 in.; front peak to crown $10\frac{3}{4}$ in.; side to crown 9 in. A spike and base were fitted on top of the helmet, in brass for rank and file and gilt for officers, the total height being $3\frac{1}{4}$ in. A chinchain of interlocking rings was fitted to the sides, the links being brass for rank and file and gilt for officers. The helmet for rank and file was of a lesser quality.

Uniform

The tunic was of khaki cloth with a stand collar and plain cuffs. There were 2 patch pockets, one on each breast, fastened by a small button. Skirts at the back were plain. Shoulders were ornamented with twisted khaki gimp boards on which was displayed the officer's rank. Privates' shoulder straps were scarlet and carried the regimental title. The tunic fastened down the front by means of 6 buttons of regimental pattern. Trousers were of khaki cloth with a scarlet welt down the outer seam of each leg. Privates wore brown leather leggings in marching order.

Accoutrements

The officer wore a brown leather waist-belt about $1\frac{1}{2}$ in. wide with sword slings 1 in. wide hanging on the left side. Officers wore a crimson sash over the left shoulder with the tassels on the right hip. Rank and file wore the 1888 pattern Slade Wallace equipment in brown leather.

Weapons

Officers carried the standard pattern Infantry sword (91 B), and other ranks were armed with the Lee-Metford rifle (95 A).

55. East Lancashire Regiment (30th and 59th). Private and Ammunition Mule, 1897

Head Dress

The head dress in the order of dress shown was the field service cap. It was of blue cloth about $4\frac{1}{2}$ in. high and $3\frac{3}{4}$ in. across the top. The crown was similar in shape to the glengarry. There was a folding peak at the front, and flaps at the side which when let down protected the ears. The lower flap fastened under the chin when worn down or across the front when worn up. The badge was worn on the left side and was a laurel wreath surmounted by a crown. In the centre was a sphinx on a tablet inscribed EGYPT above a rose. Below the rose and at the base of the laurel wreath was a scroll inscribed 'East

Lancashire'. The badge was in white metal, with only the rose in brass.

Uniform

The tunic was scarlet cloth unlined and worn on most occasions when not in full dress. There were 5 general-service buttons down the front. Below the waist at each side were pocket flaps. Cuffs were round and plain, being white as prescribed in the Cardwell reforms of 1881 for English non-Royal regiments. The shoulder straps were of the same colour as the tunic and they bore the regimental title. The collar was white, dipping at the front and ornamented on both sides with the collar badge, the rose in brass. Breeches were of khaki whipcord and worn with dark blue puttees.

Accoutrements

The 1888 pattern of equipment worn consisted of a waist-belt with 2 pouches and cross straps, with the valise worn high on the shoulders at the back. A water-bottle was slung on the right hip and a canvas haversack on the left hip.

Weapons

The rifle carried was the Lee-Enfield (95 B) the 1888-pattern bayonet (95 e) which was slowly superseding the Lee-Metford rifle (95 A).

Historical Note

The private shown is in charge of one of the ammunition mules with the reserve ammunition. 100 rounds of reserve ammunition per rifle were carried in the Small Arms wagon (S.A.A. wagon) and on 8 pack mules per regiment, there being 2 mules to each company. The whole of the ammunition allotted to Infantry battalions in India was carried on mules.

56/57. 'A' Field Battery Royal Canadian Artillery. Gunners, 1897

Head Dress

In winter dress the other ranks of the Royal Canadian Artillery wore a fur cap. The cap had a scarlet bag or fly sewn at the top and falling on the right side. When not in winter dress a black sealskin busby was worn such as that of the Royal Horse Artillery but with the addition of a yellow corded boss on the front as in the Hussars. [See *Cavalry Uniforms* by R. and C. Wilkinson-Latham (Blandford) 1968.]

Uniform

In full dress the tunic worn by the gunners was of the style of gunners of the Royal Artillery. As the busby was worn, caplines were fitted to it and around the neck of the wearer, looping and hooking on the left breast. In winter kit, as shown, a blue greatcoat was worn. This was singlebreasted and fastened at the front with 4 buttons. The collar was high and worn turned up. Around the neck a scarlet scarf was tied. Skirts of the greatcoat were turned back and fastened at the back, revealing their scarlet lining. Overalls were blue with a scarlet stripe down the outside seam and worn in both winter and summer. Short boots were worn over dark blue socks with the laces tied around the top.

Accoutrements

In review order a white buff sword belt was worn with 2 slings on the left side. As shown, only a waist-belt was worn with the straps of the snow shoes tying to the front. The snow shoes were carried on the back. Other items of equipment were carried on the limbers of the guns.

Weapons

Personal side arms were swords in review order and Martini-Henry carbines.

Historical Note

The picture shows a 9-pounder gun and limber with team mounted on a sleigh. The first permanent Artillery batteries in Canada were formed in 1871. They were armed with the 9-pounder R.M.L. (Rifled Muzzle Loader), which had a calibre of 3 in. The carriage was made almost entirely of steel. The Mk II carriage had Madras wheels, which later, towards the end of the century, were replaced by 12-pounder gun wheels when required, as the Royal Carriage Factory were unable to supply Madras wheels. During winter the guns were often mounted on sleighs, and these varied in pattern during the period 1871–1900. In this plate we show the Drury sleigh, devised by Major C. W. Drury, Royal Canadian Artillery, who at this period commanded 'A' Field Battery. Of the 3 Canadian Artillery batteries, 'A' was the senior. There were also 15 Militia batteries. The 9-pounder was replaced by the 12-pounder before the outbreak of the Boer War, 1899–1902.

58. Coldstream Guards. Guardsman, 1898

Head Dress

The white foreign-service helmet was authorised on 1 June 1877 for all ranks. The helmet was made of cork covered in white cloth in 6 seams. Peaks and side were bound in white cloth, and there was a piece of cloth 1 in. wide sewn around the helmet. This band was covered by a pugree in certain stations, such as Hong Kong, Bermuda and Malta, prior to Army Order 83 of 1896, when the pugree was prescribed for all stations abroad. The rear peak measured 12 in. from crown to edge, and the front peak measured $10\frac{3}{4}$ in. from crown to edge, while a zinc button covered in white cloth on the top of the helmet fitted into the ventilation collet. Khaki covers were worn with the helmet on certain occasions, and to prevent sunstroke a khaki curtain or neck flap was issued. On the khaki cover the identification of regiments was by means of a flash worn on the side of the helmet. In most cases the shoulder straps of the old serge frock tunics were sewn on, but otherwise regiments adopted their own identifying mark.

167

Uniform

The tunic was of khaki cloth with a stand collar and pointed cuffs, fastening down the front by means of 5 buttons in brass. There were 2 patch pockets which had a central box pleat and fastened with a small button. Khaki shoulder tabs bore the regimental title in brass. Skirts at the back were plain. Army Order 83 of 1896 altered the stand collar of the tunic to a stand-and-fall collar and lowered the pockets to 1 in. below the line of the second button. Contemporary photographs on which the illustration is based show the stand-collar tunic still being worn at this date. Trousers also of khaki cloth were worn with khaki puttees and boots. Sewn into the lining of the tunic was a card of glazed calico designated Army Form B 2067, Description card for active service. On it were written the name and number of the soldier, his rank and regiment, and his next of kin with address. When completed, the form was signed by the soldier's commanding officer. In the left side front bottom of the tunic there was sewn a field-service dressing. This consisted of a sheet of waterproof, gauze, wool, bandage and 2 safety pins packed in an extra waterproof sheet and contained in a bag of lining material. On the front of the lining bag were the following instructions: 'War Office. Medical Division. Field Service Dressing. Tear back thread in centre of long stitch. Apply first, Wool pad, second, Gauze, third, Waterproof. Fasten lightly with Bandage and Pins. If 2 wounds, put pad on one, gauze on other, and divide waterproof.' These field-service dressings were made mainly by The Darton Gibbs Co. of Oldbury. For service abroad troops were issued with spine pads and cholera belts. It was thought the soldier could suffer sunstroke if his spine were unprotected.

Accoutrements

The equipment worn was the Slade Wallace pattern of 1888 in white buff leather with brass fittings. Braces were attached to the belt at the front and, passing over the shoulders, crossed and fastened to the rear of the belt. Pouches were fitted to the belt at the front, one each side. A bayonet frog was fitted on the belt on the left side. The haversack of white canvas and the water-bottle were slung on the hip by independent straps which passed over the shoulders. The valise was worn on the back with the straps passing through D rings on the braces and fastening to double buckles on the front above the pouches. The mess-tin in oilskin cover was strapped to the rolled blanket, which fastened to the waist-belt at the back. The haversack contained emergency rations (field service). This was carried by every soldier and always produced at inspections. The label on the oval-sectioned tin which consisted of 2 tins strapped together read 'This ration is not to be opened except by order of an officer or in extremity'. It further stated that the ration was calculated to maintain strength for 36 hours if eaten in small quantities. There was a tear strip around the tins which when pulled separated them. One of the tins contained 4 oz. of concentrated beef and the other 4 oz. of cocoa. Either ration could be eaten dry or boiled in water. During the Boer War of 1899–1902 this was the only food available to the men in the exposed position at Magersfontein.

Weapons

The Army at this period were being issued with the Lee-Enfield rifle (95 B) and 1888-pattern bayonet (95 e) in place of the Lee-Metford rifle, but the changeover was by no means complete.

59. Pacific Railway Militia. Privates, 1898

Head Dress

A khaki slouch hat was worn with a blue pugree round the headband. The left side was turned up and ornamented with a large Royal Coat of Arms in brass.

Uniform

The tunic was made of khaki Nova Scotia tweed and had a blue collar, cuffs and shoulder straps. The tunic fastened down the front with 5 buttons, probably of general-service pattern. There were 4 patch pockets, one on each breast and one at each hip. The collar was decorated with a small brass grenade. Cuffs were pointed and measured 6 in. from point to edge. Trousers were also of khaki Nova Scotia tweed and were worn

with canvas leggings. The leggings measured 8½ in. high and had a leather strap and buckle sewn around the top, fastening on the outside with whipcord laces threaded through 4 eyelets.

Accoutrements

A bandolier in brown leather with small loops for cartridges was worn over the left shoulder. The waist-belt, fastening by a brass buckle, was of the same design. The private on the right in the illustration wore a kit-bag fitted on the back with leather straps which passed under the arms and over the shoulders. A haversack was carried on the left side and a water-bottle on the right.

Weapon

The militia were equipped with the Lee-Metford rifle (95 A).

Historical Note

The Pacific Railway Militia were raised in 1898–99 by the Canadian Government for the defence of the Canadian Pacific Railway. Companies of the Militia were raised at various small towns along the route. Some companies were mounted and some on foot, according to the nature of the country. At certain points along the railway route, machine-guns held in readiness could be mounted on flat cars in times of trouble.

60. Suffolk Regiment.
Privates, 1899

Head Dress

The foreign-service helmet was of white-cloth-covered cork with 6 seams and authorised for all ranks on 1 June 1877. The peaks and sides were bound in white cloth and there was a 1-in. piece of cloth encircling the helmet above the peaks. By Army Order 83 of 1896 this band was covered by a pugree on all foreign stations. A zinc button covered in white cloth was fitted on top of the helmet into the ventilation collet. Khaki covers were worn on active service, and usually worn with the curtain or neck protector as shown. The Suffolk Regiment bore on the side of the helmet the badge of a castle cut in yellow cloth, whereas other regiments unless authorised (see No. 85) wore the title on a cloth patch. The following is a Battalion Order issued by Colonel A. J. Watson dated 6 November 1899: 'Yellow cloth patches will be sewn on each side of the khaki helmet, over the ears. These are cut to form a castle. The bottom of the patch to be 4½ in. above the bottom of the helmet.' These patches were worn until 1911, when on 15 March the following order discontinued their use: 'The Commanding Officer regrets to announce that orders have been received to remove from khaki helmets the yellow castle cloth patches which have been worn by the regiment for many years both in peace and war.'

Uniform

The tunic was in khaki cloth with a stand-and-fall collar. Cuffs were plain, and the tunic fastened with 5 general-service buttons. On the chest were 2 pockets, one on each breast, the flaps fastened down with a small button. There were 2 vents at the back. Trousers were of the same material and worn with puttees. (For additional information see No. 58.) Spine pads and cholera belts were issued to all troops proceeding to South Africa.

Accoutrements

The equipment was the 1888 Slade Wallace pattern, consisting of a waist-belt, 2 cross braces, 2 ammunition pouches, a valise, rolled blanket and mess-tin in oilskin cover. A water-bottle and haversack were carried. During the Boer War, 1899–1902 the equipment was allowed to be stained and the brass fittings were not cleaned.

Weapons

Troops in the Boer War were armed with the Lee-Enfield (95 B) or the Lee-Metford (95 A).

61. Military Foot Police. Sergeant and Corporal, 1904

Head Dress

The corporal shown in the illustration wore the regulation cork helmet covered in blue cloth, the cloth having 2 seams at each side. Peaks at the back and front were both rounded and bound in black leather. A ¾-in. band of blue cloth was sewn top and bottom around the headband above the peaks. The chinchain was of interlocking brass rings backed with leather and attached to the helmet on 2 brass rosettes. The top of the helmet was ornamented with a cross piece and spike in brass. The helmet plate was the universal star plate surmounted by a crown and die struck in brass. In the centre was the Garter belt with motto, within which was the Royal cipher E.R. VII. The forage cap was of blue cloth worn with a red cover for the top, giving the corps their nickname of the 'Red Caps'. The peak was of black patent leather with a chinstrap worn above and attached at either side of the peak by small buttons. The badge design was of a laurel wreath surrounding the Royal cipher, the whole surmounted by a crown. A scroll underneath bore the title 'Military Police'.

Uniform

The tunic was of blue cloth with scarlet collar and pointed cuffs; the leading edge of the tunic was also piped in scarlet cloth. Cuffs measured about 3½ in. from the point to the edge and were bound all round in gold cord for sergeants and worsted cord for other ranks, terminating in ornamental knots at the point. Shoulders were ornamented with gold cord for sergeants and yellow cord for other ranks. Tunic skirts were ornamented with 2 slashed flaps piped in scarlet and with a central line of scarlet cloth between them.

The flaps had 3 buttons on each. The tunic was fastened by 9 brass buttons bearing the design of the Royal cipher surmounted by a crown. Trousers were of blue cloth with a 2-in. scarlet stripe running down the outside seam of both legs.

Accoutrements

A brown leather belt was worn fastened with a brass buckle. A whistle and chain were worn, the chain attached to the second button from the top and the whistle fitting into a small pocket inside the tunic.

Historical Note

The Corps of Military Foot Police was recruited from other corps and regiments of the British Army. The man had to be of good character and have at least one good conduct badge and have 4 years' service. There are no privates in the corps, each man transferred being raised to the rank of corporal.

62. Northamptonshire Regiment (48th and 58th). Officer and Bugler, 1906

Head Dress

The forage cap was made of material to match the service dress and was of cotton yarn proofed. The wide cloth-covered peak was set at an angle of about 60 degrees and carried well back to protect the temples. The cap was 9¼ in. across the top (fitting 21¾ in. in circumference), the cap to be ⅛ in. smaller or larger in diameter for every ¼ in. variation in head size.

A brown leather chinstrap was fitted to the cap at the sides by 2 small regimental-pattern buttons. Buttons were bronzed when worn with service dress and had the design within a scroll inscribed Northamptonshire Regiment of the castle and key. Above the castle was a scroll inscribed GIBRALTAR. Beneath the castle and key was another scroll inscribed TALAVERA. On the lower bend of the wreath was a scroll with the word 'Northamptonshire'. In the cap buttons the regimental name was omitted.

Uniform

The jacket was of special mixture serge and the same colour as that issued to other ranks. It was single-breasted with 4 pockets. Breast pockets were 6½ in. wide and 7½ in. deep, with a box pleat in the centre 2¼ in. wide. Flaps were fastened with a regimental-pattern button. Pockets on the jacket below the waist were 9¼ in. wide at the top and 10½ in. at the bottom, and 8 in. deep. There were 5 buttons of regimental pattern down the front. The collar was noted in the dress regulations as being 'turn down (Prussian)' and could be adjusted by a tab with 2 button holes under the collar. There was a 2¼-in. expanding pleat down the centre of the back, sewn down below the 2¼-in. waist band. Cuffs were round with a 3-pointed flap sewn on, edged in chevron tape and carrying badges of rank. There were also a band or bands of chevron tape around the cuff, the number depending on rank:

Second-lieutenants and lieutenants	1 row
Captains	2 rows
Majors	3 rows with tracing braid between
Lieutenant-colonel	3 rows with 4 rows of tracing braid between
Colonel	4 rows with 5 rows of tracing braid

Shoulder straps were as for rank and file. Breeches were of the same serge mixture as the jacket. Puttees were woollen and matched the rest of the uniform. Other ranks wore a similar jacket with the regimental name on a flash on the shoulders. They also wore trousers, as distinct from officers' breeches.

Accoutrements

The officer wore the Sam Browne belt with 2 braces over the shoulders, crossing at the back and fastening to the waist-belt. A sword frog was attached to the left side and an ammunition pouch and revolver holster on the right. A lanyard attached to the butt of the weapon was looped around the neck. Over the left shoulder was a strap for the water-bottle, which was suspended on the right hip by a belt. On the left hip, suspended from the right shoulder by another strap, was the haversack. A binocular case was carried on the right hip from a belt over the left shoulder. The bugler wore a waist-belt with frog and a water-bottle and haversack.

Weapons

The officer was armed with a revolver (Appendix 2) and sword in a leather-covered scabbard with a metal chape (91 B).

63. 2nd Prince of Wales' Own Gurkha Rifles (The Sirmoor Rifles). Subadar-Major and Rifleman, 1906

Head Dress

The head dress was in the shape of a pillbox cap in green cloth with a red-and-black-diced band around the bottom of the cap. The top was decorated with a red worsted pompom. On the front was the regimental badge in white metal. This was the Prince of Wales' feathers with the number 2 beneath. A black leather chinstrap was fitted at the sides.

Uniform

The tunic for service dress as illustrated was in dark rifle green cloth, fastened down the front with 8 regimental-pattern horn buttons. The collars of both the Subadar-Major and the rifleman were in dark green with the lower part edged in a red welt. There were 4 pockets, 2 side pockets and 1 on each breast, with buttons only on the breast pockets. The officer's tunic had twisted black cord shoulder straps with the ranking in black on a red backing. The rifleman's shoulder straps were in the same colour as the tunic and bore the regimental designation in white metal. The back of the cuff had 3 small buttons for riflemen but plain for the officers. Trousers were also in the dark green cloth and worn with black puttees.

Accoutrements

The other ranks' waist-belt was in black leather with a snake-buckle fastening in white metal. A bayonet frog was carried on the left side and the kukri was carried on the right. The officer's waist-belt was in black patent leather fastened on the front with a silver plate carrying the regimental badge in silver. There were 2 sword slings hanging on the left side. Over the left shoulder was worn a black patent leather crossbelt suspending at the back a leather pouch. The belt was ornamented with a silver lion head, chain and whistle.

Weapons

Other ranks were armed with the Lee-Metford rifle (95 A) and bayonet (95 e). Officers carried the rifle-pattern sword in a steel scabbard (91 C).

Historical Note

The distinctive red-and-black dicing to the cap was said to have been introduced by a Scottish colonel. Unfortunately the reason has been lost in obscurity. Some time in the 1900s an attempt was made to introduce pugrees for Gurkhas, but this never came about. For the Waziristan Campaign of 1901 they were issued with the felt slouch hat which is now the head dress worn by the Gurkha regiments. In 1906 the regimental title was changed to 2nd King

Edward's Own Gurkha Rifles (The Sirmoor Rifles). The badge now was of a new design incorporating the Imperial cipher.

64. Honourable Artillery Company (Infantry). Officer and Private, 1909

Head Dress

A black bearskin cap was worn between $8\frac{1}{2}$ and 10 in. high, depending on the height of the wearer. The chin-chain was of tapering brass interlocking rings lined in black leather. The bearskin cap worn by sergeants and other ranks was of the same design but not so high.

Uniform

The tunic was of scarlet cloth with blue collar, cuffs and shoulder straps. The collar was laced and embroidered in silver and decorated with a grenade. Cuffs were round and $3\frac{1}{2}$ in. deep with embroidery around the top. In addition, the cuffs had a slashed panel in blue cloth adorned with silver embroidery and buttons. Buttons had the design of the Royal cipher reversed and interlaced, surmounted by a crown with a grenade beneath the cipher in the centre. The skirts were ornamented with a scarlet flap on each side reaching to within $\frac{1}{2}$ in. of the bottom of the skirt and adorned with silver embroidery and buttons. There were 2 buttons at the waist above the skirt. Leading edges of tunic, collar, cuffs and flaps were piped in white cloth $\frac{1}{4}$ in. wide. The blue cloth shoulder straps were embroidered with 2 rows of silver pearl embroidery around the edge and bore the rank of the wearer. The front of the tunic fastened by 9 equidistant buttons. For privates the tunic was cut and decorated in similar fashion to that of the Grenadier Guards private except that buttons were in white metal and shoulder straps bore the title 'H.A.C.' in white embroidery. The officer's trousers were blue with a stripe $2\frac{1}{2}$ in. wide down the outer seam of each leg, and the rank and file had blue trousers with a scarlet welt on the outer seams.

Accoutrements

The private wore a white buff waist-belt with a buff bayonet frog on the left side. The buckle was in brass, with a grenade and cipher in the centre surrounded by the title 'Honourable Artillery Company'. The officer is wearing the state sash in crimson and silver, with tassels on the left side. The sword belt was worn under the tunic, with slings hanging on the left side.

Weapons

The officer's sword was similar to that of the Grenadier Guards, but the embossing on the blade differed (91 G). The men were armed with the Lee-Enfield rifle (95 B) and 1888-pattern bayonet (95 e).

Historical Note

In the reign of William IV the Honourable Artillery Company were given permission to wear uniform similar to that of Grenadier Guards, but with silver lace instead of gold.

174

A further change took place in 1855 when Infantry battalions were allowed to replace the shako by the bearskin caps without plume.

65. 10th (Scottish) Battalion The King's (Liverpool) Regiment. Officer and Sergeant, 1909

Head Dress

The head dress for both officers and men was the glengarry cap prescribed in 1852 for Highland and Scottish Regiments. It was blue with a diced border for the battalion, although some other Highland regiments had no diced border. The cap was bound around the lower edge with black silk, which terminated at the back, the 2 ends hanging down. A black silk rosette was sewn on to the left side, on which was fitted the badge. Behind the rosette was fitted a black cock feather. On the top of the cap was a red toorie. The plain glengarry without diced border had been adopted for all regiments of the Army as an undress cap in 1874.

Uniform

As this was a Scottish battalion the doublet was worn by both officers and other ranks. It was a drab colour with red collar and cuffs. The collar was edged around the top and the front in silver lace. Cuffs were gauntlet-shaped, with silver lace around the top and down the back seam, and had 3 silver braid button loops and silver buttons on each. The doublet had 7 buttons down the front, with the leading edge piped in

red. The Inverness skirts were piped in red around the edge, as were the flaps. Flaps were ornamented with 3 silver braid loops and silver buttons of regimental pattern. On both shoulders a twisted-silver-cord shoulder board displayed the wearer's rank in gold embroidery. On the left shoulder was worn the plaid in Forbes tartan, held in place by a large silver plaid brooch with the regimental badge in the centre. The kilt was also in Forbes tartan. The sporran belt was brown leather. The sporran was silver-topped, engraved and fitted with the regimental badge. The hair was grey, with two black tassels. Hose-tops were red with a criss-cross pattern, and spats were white, fastened on the outside with black buttons.

The other ranks' doublet was of the same design and colour, except that collar, cuffs and skirts were decorated with white tape and braid in place of the silver worn by officers. Shoulder straps were red edged in white. Both officers and other ranks wore collar badges of regimental pattern. The sporran worn by the other ranks had a black top edged in white metal, with the regimental badge fitted in the centre of the top. The hair was grey, with the 2 tassels in black. The regimental badge was the cross of St Andrew superimposed with a half circle at the top bearing the words 'Liverpool Scottish' and a half wreath of thistles at the bottom. In the centre was a prancing horse surmounting a scroll which bore the words 'The King's'.

Accoutrements

Officers wore a brown leather cross-belt with pouch. On the front in silver was a plate of regimental pattern surmounted by a crown. Waist-belt and sword slings were also in brown leather, and the belt plate or locket was in silver of regimental pattern. Other ranks wore a brown leather waist-belt with silver clasp.

Weapons

Officers wore the claymore (90 A) and the skean-dhu. Other ranks carried the long Lee-Enfield rifle (95 B) and short bayonet (not illustrated).

Historical Note

The unit was formed in April 1900 and given the title of the 8th (Scottish) Volunteer Battalion of the King's Liverpool Regiment. In 1908 it became the 10th Battalion. In 1937 it transferred to the Queen's Own Cameron Highlanders and was renamed the Liverpool Scottish.

66. Royal Army Medical Corps. Warrant Officer Class II and Orderly, 1910

Head Dress

The helmet worn by the W.O. II was the regulation cork helmet introduced by General Order 40 of May 1878. The cork body was covered in blue cloth and was seamed twice on either side. The front rounded peak was bound in leather $\frac{1}{8}$ in. wide, the binding continuing round the sides and back peak. Above the peaks and

around the helmet was a cloth band $\frac{3}{4}$ in. wide sewn top and bottom. The chinchain was of brass interlocking rings backed with leather and attached to the helmet at either side on brass rosettes. The top of the helmet was ornamented with a brass cross piece indented with roses at the 4 terminations and surmounted by a brass ball in a leaf socket. The helmet plate was an 8-pointed star surmounted by a crown and decorated either side with a laurel-leaf spray. In the centre was a Garter belt with the motto *Honi soit qui mal y pense*. In the centre of the Garter belt was a red cross. The orderly in service dress wore the regulation forage cap in khaki yarn proofed cloth with a wide peak set at an angle of about 60 degrees. A brown leather chinstrap was fitted at either side and rested above the peak. The badge was the design of a laurel wreath surmounted by a crown, with in the centre the rod of Escalapius with a serpent entwined. At the bottom of the wreath was a scroll bearing the title 'Royal Army Medical Corps'.

Uniform

The tunic was of blue cloth with dark cherry collar and cuffs and buttoning down the front with 7 buttons. Buttons had the design of a laurel wreath with the rod of Escalapius and serpent in the centre with the title 'Royal Army Medical Corps' around the wreath. The collar was edged in Russia braid and gold lace, and was further decorated with the corps badge already described in gilt. Cuffs were pointed and measured $3\frac{1}{2}$ in.

deep from the top of the point to the edge. The cuff top was decorated in Russia braid, terminating in a crow's-foot knot at the apex of the point. The leading edge of the front of the tunic was piped in dark cherry, as were the slashed panels at the back of the tunic. The centre line at the rear was also in cherry. Panels were further ornamented with 2 buttons, with 2 more at the waist. Shoulders were decorated with twisted gold cords. Trousers were of blue cloth, with dark cherry-red stripes down the outside seams. The orderly in the illustration is wearing the regulation service dress. The tunic was of khaki cloth with a turn-down collar and fastened down the front with 5 buttons. There were 4 pockets on the jacket, the 2 on the chest having box pleats, the 2 below the waist being plain. Trousers were of plain khaki, and brown leather gaiters were worn.

Accoutrements

The W.O. II wore a white buff sword belt with 2 slings, 1 long and 1 short. The belt was fastened with a gilt universal pattern locket. The belt worn by other ranks was of the white Slade Wallace pattern with universal brass locket.

Weapon

The W.O. II carried a brass hilted sword in steel scabbard. This pattern was peculiar to the Corps from 1892 to 1934 (91 A).

67. Army Pay Corps.
Sergeant and Private, 1910

Head Dress

The sergeant in the illustration wore the regulation Home pattern helmet introduced in May 1878. The body was made of cork covered in blue cloth, with 2 seams each side. There were 2 peaks, 1 at the back and 1 at the front, both covered in blue cloth and bound all round the lower edge in black leather. Above the peaks and circling the helmet was a blue cloth band sewn top and bottom. The chin-chain was of interlocking brass rings backed with leather and attached to the helmet on 2 brass rosettes. A $3\frac{1}{2}$-in. spike and base was fitted on top of the helmet, ornamented with a rosette in the centre and rosettes at the end of the cross piece. The star plate measured 5 in. in height and $4\frac{1}{2}$ in. in width and was of die-stamped brass. The plate was an 8-pointed star surmounted by a crown. On the rays of the star was a laurel wreath around the Garter belt and motto *Honi soit qui mal y pense*. Within the Garter belt were the letters 'A.P.C.' intertwined. The private shown wore the forage cap of blue cloth with yellow piping around the top and above and below the band. The peak was of black patent leather set at an angle of 45 degrees. A black leather chinstrap was fitted to the cap by 2 small buttons either side of the peak. The badge on the front was in brass and had the letters 'A.P.C.' intertwined and surmounted by a crown.

Uniform

The tunic was in dark blue cloth with yellow cloth collar and cuffs. Cuffs were pointed and measured about 3½ in. from point to cuff. The collar, about 1½ in. high, was piped around the bottom edge in yellow cloth, which continued down the leading edge of the tunic. Shoulder straps were in blue cloth edged in yellow and decorated with the corps title. Skirts at the back of the tunic had 2 slashed panels edged in yellow, with 2 buttons on each and a button above each at the waist. There was also a central line between the panels. The tunic fastened with 7 buttons. Trousers were in blue cloth, with a double yellow stripe down the outer seam of each leg.

Accoutrements

The waist-belt was in buff leather, fastened on the front with a brass universal pattern locket.

Historical Note

The corps were granted the title Royal for their services during the First World War, 1914–18.

68. 4th Battalion Royal Scots (Lothian Regiment). Private and Bugler, 1910

Head Dress

The head dress worn by both the 4th and 5th Battalions Royal Scots was the rifle busby. It was made of black dyed sealskin and measured 5 in.

high at the front and back, rising to 6 in. in the centre. The crown was of rifle green cloth. On the top front of the cap was a black corded boss, behind which was fitted the plume in a spring holder. The plume was dark green with a plaited holder around the base. Sets of black worsted cord lines were fitted to the busby, one at each side, with the section across the front plaited. The chinstrap was of black patent leather. The officer's busby was of the same design, but the body was of black lambskin.

Uniform

The tunic, collar and cuffs were of rifle green cloth. Cuffs were pointed and edged in black worsted tape. The collar was edged around the top in black worsted tape, and around the base of the collar there was a line of black piping which continued down the leading edge of the tunic. There were 7 buttons down the front. Shoulder straps were green piped in black and bore the regimental title. Trousers were also of dark rifle green cloth. The officer's uniform was of the rifle pattern with the frogged tunic.

Accoutrements

In full dress a black leather waist-belt and one pouch was worn. In service dress the complete equipment of the web 1908 pattern or the leather 1903 was worn. Officers in full dress had the patent leather crossbelt and pouch; the crossbelt had a lion head, chain and whistle separated by the regimental plate.

178

Weapons

Rank and file were armed with the Lee-Enfield rifle (95 B) and 1888-pattern bayonet (95 e), and officers carried the rifle pattern sword (91 C).

Historical Note

The battalion was formerly the City of Edinburgh Rifle Volunteer Corps, and was the successor to the 'Town Guard', the Trained Bands, the Edinburgh Volunteers and others. The Honorary Colonel of the 4th Battalion was by ancient custom the Lord Provost of Edinburgh.

69. 15th Ludhiana Sikhs.
Colour Party, 1910

Head Dress

The lungi was of red-and-yellow striped cloth and tied around the head as shown. It was ornamented on the front with a regimental-pattern badge in white metal.

Uniform

The tunic was of scarlet cloth for Indian V.C.O.s (Viceroy Commissioned Officers) and also for colour sergeants and other ranks. Collar and cuffs were of the regimental face colour, which for the 15th Ludhiana Sikhs was green. The collar of the officer's tunic was edged in gold lace with a trace of Russia braid at the base. The cuffs were round, edged in white and decorated with a slashed flap also in green cloth with white edging. The flap or panel was ornamented with 3 gold-lace button loops and buttons for officers and buttons only for other ranks. The tunic fastened down the front by means of 8 regimental-pattern buttons. The front of the tunic was further decorated with a panel each side of the closing in green cloth, edged in white for other ranks and gold lace for officers. Skirts were decorated with 2 panels edged in white and ornamented with buttons. Trousers were in blue, with a scarlet welt down the outer seam of each leg. White spats were worn.

Accoutrements

Colour sergeants wore a brown leather belt with 2 brown leather pouches each side at the front. Officers wore a crimson sash around the waist, with tassels hanging on the left side. The colour belts were in brown leather with gilt fittings.

Weapons

Officers carried the regulation Indian Army pattern Infantry sword (91 B). Rank and file were armed with the S.M.L.E. (95 C).

Colours

The King's Colour was of the usual pattern of Union flag with a central circle bearing the regimental title. The Regimental Colour was in the face colour and bore the title in a circle within a wreath, with the regimental battle honours on each side.

70. 101st Grenadiers.
Bugler and Sepoys, 1910

Head Dress

The head dress worn was the pugree tied around the head with a white fringe at the top. On the front of the head dress was worn a brass grenade badge. The kullah or close-fitting pointed cap was red.

Uniform

A scarlet blouse was worn with scarlet collar and cuffs. The bottom edge of the collar was piped in white. The piping continued down the front in 2 lines, 1 each side of brass buttons fastening the blouse. The blouse reached to just above the knees, with a vent at each side. Cuffs were pointed and piped in white. Shoulder straps were in white cloth. Trousers were loosely cut and in blue serge cloth, with a scarlet welt down the outside seam of each leg. The spats were in white, fastening on the outside with buttons. Around the waist was worn a cummerbund in white cloth with red stripes. The bugler wore body cords as shown.

Accoutrements

A brown leather waist-belt was worn holding the bayonet frog on the left hip. In marching order the full equipment was worn, consisting of pouches, haversack, water-bottle, etc.

Weapons

This regiment was armed with the Lee-Enfield rifle (95 B) and 1888-pattern bayonet (95 e).

Historical Note

The 1st Bombay Native Infantry had been designated Grenadiers in 1824.

71. Army Motor Reserve.
Officers, 1911

Head Dress

The forage cap was of a drab green cloth, with a green cloth welt around the top. The top of the cap was about $9\frac{1}{4}$ in. in diameter and about $21\frac{3}{4}$ in. in circumference. A green cloth band $1\frac{3}{4}$ in. went around the headband. The black patent leather peak, set into the cap at an angle of 45 degrees, was $1\frac{3}{4}$ in. deep in the centre. The chin-strap was of black patent leather $\frac{3}{8}$ in. wide and buttoned to the cap with 2 buttons placed immediately behind the corners of the peak. The badge of gilt metal was of the design of an arrow superimposed with a scroll bearing the motto *Subito*.

Uniform

The tunic was in drab green cloth with dark green collar and cuffs. The collar was ornamented with $\frac{5}{8}$ in. lace along the top and gold Russia braid at the base of the collar. The collar badge, fitted to each side, was similar to the cap badge, but smaller in size. Cuffs were pointed and ornamented with $\frac{5}{8}$ in. lace around the top. There was a tracing of Russia braid above, terminating in an ornamental knot. The tunic fastened down the front with 8 gilt buttons bearing the initials 'A.M.R.' with the 'A' centred above the other 2 letters, the 'M' on the left and the 'R' on the right.

Beneath the initials was a scroll with the word *Subito*. Skirts were closed behind and edged in green cloth on the closing seam, with a 2-pointed slashed flap on each side decorated with a button at each point. Collar, leading edge and slashes were edged with a $\frac{1}{4}$-in.-wide green welt. Shoulders were decorated with twisted-gold-cord boards lined in green, which were fastened with a small button and bore the rank of the officer. Trousers were of the same cloth as the tunic and had a green welt running down the outside seam of each leg.

Accoutrements

The waist-belt was of gold lace and about $1\frac{1}{2}$ in. wide, with a locket at the front and 2 sword slings on the left side. The outer circle of the locket bore the title 'Army Motor Reserve', with inside the circle the arrow and scroll with the motto *Subito*. The crossbelt was of gold lace, with a green train in the centre. The pouch was of black leather and ornamented with an edging of gold lace, with in the centre on the flap an arrow-and-scroll badge as worn on the cap.

Weapon

Officers carried the standard pattern Infantry sword (91 B).

Historical Note

The Army Motor Reserve was formed in 1910 by Colonel Challoner Knox from the 5th Militia Battalion The Royal Irish Regiment. The 5th

Battalion's previous title was the Kilkenny Militia.

72/73. Royal Scots Fusiliers (21st). Colour Party, 1912

Head Dress

The officer's cap was made of either black bearskin or black racoon skin and measured about 8–10 in. high, depending on the height of the officer. A white cut-feather plume worn on the right side fitted into a two-flame gilt socket. The plume measured $6\frac{1}{2}$ in. high. The front of the cap was ornamented with a grenade badge in gilt, with the Royal Coat of Arms on the ball. The chinchain was of interlocking gilt rings backed with black leather and velvet. Caps worn by colour sergeants and rank and file were smaller and made of black dyed sealskin. The plume was in horsehair, and the grenade was die-stamped in brass.

Uniform

The doublet was of scarlet cloth, with collar and cuffs of the face colour, which for the Royal Scots Fusiliers was blue. The collar was laced along the top with $\frac{5}{8}$ in. gold thistle-pattern lace and around the base of the collar with gold Russia braid. The gauntlet cuffs measured $3\frac{1}{2}$ in. deep in front and 6 in. at the back, and were edged in $\frac{5}{8}$ in. gold thistle-pattern lace round the top and down the back seam. Cuffs were further ornamented with 3 gold button loops and gilt buttons. The doublet fastened down the front by means of 8 regimental-pattern buttons, there being also 2 buttons at the waist behind. Buttons bore the design of the thistle surmounted by a crown. The Inverness skirts were as follows: the 2 on the front measured 8 in. deep and had pocket flaps 7½ in. deep, the ones at the back were slightly shorter, with the tongues at the rear measuring 7 in. Front and side flaps were ornamented with 3 gold-braid button loops and regimental-pattern buttons. Collar, leading edge, skirts and flaps were piped in white cloth ¼ in. wide. Shoulders were ornamented with twisted gold shoulder cords of the universal pattern lined in scarlet with a small regimental-pattern button at the top and displaying the badge or badges of rank. The trews were of Black Watch tartan. The doublet worn by colour sergeants and rank and file was also in scarlet cloth and of the same basic design. Shoulder straps were scarlet and ornamented with the regimental designation and grenade. Loops on cuffs and skirts were in white tape, and cuffs were also edged in white tape. The badge of colour sergeants was worn on the right arm. This was crossed Union flags surmounted by a crown above a 3-bar chevron in gold lace.

Accoutrements

Colour sergeants had a crimson sash over the right shoulder, with tassels hanging on the left hip. Officers wore a netted crimson sash over their left shoulders. Also over the left shoulder was the colour belt with gilt fittings. A white buff leather sword belt was worn over the right shoulder, with 2 slings hanging on the left hip. The belt was fastened at the chest by a crossbelt plate of regimental pattern. The plate of burnished gilt brass bore the design in silver of a thistle within a crowned Garter belt with the motto *Honi soit qui mal y pense*. At the bottom of the circle was a small Maltese Cross. Below the Garter belt was a scroll with the title 'Royal Scots Fusiliers', below which was a smaller scroll with the date 1678. Colour sergeants wore the regulation pattern Slade Wallace belt with bayonet frog, the remainder of this pattern of equipment now being obsolete.

Weapons

Colour sergeants had the S.M.L.E. rifle (95 C) and bayonet (95 f). Officers carried the claymore (90 A).

Historical Note

The Colours shown in the illustration were presented to the Royal Scots Fusiliers by the Duchess of Connaught when the regiment was stationed at Aldershot in 1895 and saw continuous service with the regiment until laid up in 1950. The next Colours were presented in 1950 in Germany by Lord Trenchard, who held the honorary rank of major-general. The Royal Scots Fusiliers were amalgamated on 20 January 1959 with the Highland Light Infantry to form The Royal Highland Fusiliers.

74. Royal Flying Corps.
Officer and Sergeant, 1913

Head Dress

The Royal Flying Corps from their beginning wore the field service cap as shown. This cap was similar in shape to the glengarry worn by Scottish regiments. The field service cap was khaki, matching the rest of the uniform, and was worn by both officers and other ranks. It measured about $4\frac{1}{2}$ in. high and was $3\frac{3}{4}$ in. across the top. At the front was a peak which with the sides could be folded down for added protection from the wind and cold. The side flaps fastened down under the chin with 2 small corps buttons, but when worn up as shown appeared on the front of the cap. Buttons bore the crown and albatross with the letters 'R.F.C.' beneath. The cap badge was in bronze and consisted of a wreath of laurels surrounding the monogram 'R.F.C.', the whole surmounted by a crown.

Uniform

The tunic was of khaki cloth and double-breasted, fastening on the right side, though no buttons were visible. The collar was of the pattern described in regulations for Infantry service dress, namely fall down, and on the officer's tunic this was ornamented with collar badges of the same design as the cap badge but of smaller size. Other ranks and non-commissioned officers did not wear collar badges, but instead wore shoulder titles on both shoulders. These were in white worsted embroidery on a blue ground with the name 'Royal Flying Corps'. The ranking on the officer's tunic was worn on the shoulder straps, unlike his counterparts in the other arms of the service, who wore theirs on the cuff (excepting general officers). Cuffs of the tunic had straps for tightening around the wrist when required. Both officers and other ranks wore breeches and puttees doing up from top to bottom. Officers wore brown boots and other ranks black.

Accoutrements

Officers wore the Sam Browne belt of brown leather $2\frac{1}{8}$ in. wide and of length to suit the wearer. Only one brace was worn, usually about 28 in. long, but varying according to the wearer. A brown leather holster was fitted on the right-hand side. As can be seen from the illustration, the sergeant wore a brown leather waistbelt with the holster on the right side. A lanyard attached to the butt of the revolver looped around the neck.

Weapons

Officers, warrant officers and sergeants carried revolvers (Appendix 2).

75. Royal Scots (Lothian Regiment) (1st). Officer and Bugler, 1914

Head Dress

The head dress worn by the Royal Scots and the King's Own Scottish Borderers was the Kilmarnock bonnet. It was introduced in 1904 and replaced the blue cloth helmet worn since 1878. The bonnet was made of blue nap cloth, with a diced head-band of red, white and green, the bottom edge being bound in black silk. A black silk rosette was fitted to the left front side, and there was also a black silk bow at the back of the bonnet. A red ball tuft topped the head dress. The badge, worn on the black silk rosette, was the star of the Order of the Thistle with, in the centre in gilt, a raised circle inscribed *Nemo me impune lacessit*. Within the circle, backed with green enamel, was a thistle in gilt. A black-cock's feather was fitted behind the silk rosette on the left front. The rank-and-file Kilmarnock bonnet was of the same pattern but of lesser quality. The badge for the rank and file was the star of the Order of the Thistle; in the centre St Andrew and Cross, below which was a scroll inscribed 'Royal Scots'. The star was in white metal and the centre design in brass.

Uniform

The doublet was of scarlet cloth with blue facings. The collar was edged all round in gold lace of thistle pattern and further ornamented with collar badges of thistles in gold embroidery with the stalks pointing inwards. Gauntlet cuffs also in the face colour of blue measured $3\frac{1}{2}$ in. deep at the front and 6 in. at the back, edged in gold lace round the top and down the back seams. Cuffs were decorated with 3 buttons and button loops of gold braid. Buttons were in gilt and bore the design of the star of the Order of the Thistle and

below the badge the name 'The Royal Scots'. The Inverness skirts, the name given to the flaps at the back and front of the doublet, had pocket flaps on the front and back side ones. Between the back flaps and directly below the 2 buttons at the waist were 2 small tongue-like flaps. These were piped in white and the pocket flaps decorated with 3 buttons and gold braid loops. Shoulders were decorated with twisted-gold-cord shoulder boards which displayed ranking in silver embroidery. The rank-and-file doublet was of the same pattern but of lesser quality. Shoulders had straps bearing the regimental title in white embroidery. The bugler wore the doublet of the Corps of Drums, namely the cuffs, and seams were decorated with drummer's tape, as was the collar. Shoulders carried wing-pattern epaulettes, also decorated with drummer's tape.

Trews of the Lothian tartan were worn by all ranks.

The bugler had the further decoration of plaited cords worn on the doublet.

Accoutrements

Officers wore a crimson net sash over the left shoulder, with 2 tassels hanging at the right side. A white buff leather crossbelt was worn over the right shoulder, with 2 rings connected by a small strap of white buff on the left waist. To the rings were attached the sword slings, 1 long, 1 short. The crossbelt fastened on the chest with a regimental-pattern plate of burnished gilt metal with the star of the Order of the Thistle in the centre in silver and gilt, the centre backed with green enamel. Below the star was a scroll with the words 'The Royal Scots'. The waist-belt was of gold thistle pattern lace on leather 1¾ in. wide, fastening at the front with a gilt rectangular plate decorated with the star of the Order of the Thistle. The bugler's waist-belt was of white buff leather, as were the rank-and-file belts. The plate was rectangular with the regimental badge and not the universal-pattern locket worn by the rest of the rank and file. Cords of red, yellow and blue worsted with tassels at the end were worn on the doublet. The bugle of copper and brass was slung by cords of the same pattern.

Weapons

The officer carried the claymore (90 A) in a nickel-plated scabbard. The bugler wore the bayonet or bugler's sword (90 G).

76. Highland Light Infantry (71st and 74th).
   Officer and R.S.M., 1914

Head Dress

The shako worn by officers, R.S.M. and rank and file was adopted in 1862. It was of blue cloth, 4 in. high at the front and 6½ in. at the back. The crown was 6 in. long and 5½ in. across. Around the bottom edge and above the peak was a diced band of white, red and dark green. The peak was horizontal and of black japanned leather, as was the chinstrap. At the top front of the shako was a corded

boss on which was fitted a gilt thistle. The caplines were plaited in the section that fell down above the peak. The lines encircled the cap, fitting at either side on a bronze ornament with a small hook. At the back was a further bronze ornament which covered a small ventilation hole. Above the corded boss on the top front of the shako was fitted a green pom-pom in an ornamental gilt holder. The shako plate was of silver, as was the star of the Order of the Thistle, upon which was fitted a bugle horn, with in it the monogram H.L.I. in gilt. Below this was the elephant with the battle honour ASSAYE on a scroll. The crown above the bugle horn on the shako plate was as represented in the collar of the Order of the Star of India, and the cap of the crown was in crimson velvet. Officers were distinguished by lace on the shako. Colonels and lieutenant-colonels had 2 rows of ⅝-in. thistle-pattern lace around the top of the shako, and majors one row. Below the rank of major the shako was plain as shown. The shakos of the other ranks followed this design except in regard to quality, and the shako plate was stamped in one piece out of white metal.

Uniform

Being a Scottish regiment, a scarlet doublet was worn with collar and cuffs of the regimental face colour, which in this case was buff. The collar was edged in gold lace according to rank. Cuffs were described as gauntlet cuffs and edged in gold lace according to rank, with 3 gold-lace loops and buttons on each. Buttons were of regimental pattern: gilt convex and with the same design as the shako plate. There were 8 buttons down the front of the doublet, and the leading edge was piped in white. At the waist at the back were 2 buttons. Inverness skirts, the name given to the flaps at the front and back of highland doublets, had pocket flaps on the two at the front and back. The two smaller flaps directly at the back were plain. Pocket flaps had 3 loops of gold braid and a regimental-pattern button on each. Skirts and flaps were piped in white and also lined in white. On the collar on each side was fitted a regimental-pattern collar badge. Twisted-gold-cord epaulettes were fitted to both shoulders. A shoulder plaid was worn tied around the body once and pinned at the left shoulder with a plaid brooch in silver. The plaid hung down from the left shoulder. A crimson sash was worn over the left shoulder under the plaid and was described in Dress Regulations as being of highland pattern. It was 15 in. wide in the centre and tapered to 7 in. at the commencement of the fringes. The caplines were of black silk cord with acorn ends and fell from the back of the shako, looped around the collar and hooked below it to the left side. Trousers, or trews as they were termed, were in MacKenzie tartan for both battalions. The R.S.M. wore a doublet of scarlet similar to the rank and file, but with gold lace on the collar and cuffs. Also gold-cord epaulettes were worn.

Skirts were decorated in the same manner as the doublet of the officers, but in white piping only.

Accoutrements

A white buff crossbelt was worn with two slings hanging from two rings on the left side. The belt was 3 in. wide and the slings 1 in. The belt was fastened on the chest with a regimental-pattern belt plate. In the Highland Light Infantry this was a mat gilt plate with a replica badge as worn on the shako. The waist-belt was of leather faced with thistle-pattern gold lace and had a gilt plate of regimental pattern.

Weapons

The officer carried the claymore (90 A) in a steel scabbard with the cross hilt. The R.S.M. carried the sword with full basket hilt. The dirk in the Highland Light Infantry had all-gilt fittings with polished gem stones as finials of the grips of the large knife and the companion small knife and fork. The badge of the regiment was affixed to the mount of the scabbard.

77. Royal Irish Rifles (83rd and 86th). Sergeant and Rifleman, 1914

Head Dress

The busby of black dyed sealskin measured 5 in. high, back and front rising to 6 in. in the centre. The crown was of rifle green cloth. A black worsted set of caplines was fitted to the cap, the front portion being plaited and sewn to the cap. On the top centre front of the cap was a black corded boss ornamented with a sphinx over the word EGYPT, all in bronze. This was above a stringed bugle horn. Below the boss on the fur of the cap was the badge of a harp surmounted by a crown with the motto *Quis separabit* all in bronze. The officer's cap was in lambskin, and the green cloth top was ornamented with tracings in black braid. Badges were in silver.

Uniform

Tunic, collar and cuffs were of dark rifle green cloth. Cuffs were decorated with a point of black worsted lace. The top and bottom of the collar and the leading edge were piped in black. The tunic fastened down the front by means of 7 black buttons bearing the stringed bugle horn and crown. Skirts at the back of the tunic were ornamented with slashed panels piped in black and decorated with 2 buttons on each flap. Shoulder straps of rifle green cloth and edged all round in black tape bore the regimental title. Trousers were of dark green cloth, which appeared nearly black. Officers wore the frogged tunic in dark green, with black cord frogging on the chest.

Accoutrements

The waist-belt worn in full dress was in black leather fastened by a snake buckle. A black leather bayonet frog was worn on the left side, and in certain cases one black leather pouch was worn on the right side. Equipment for service dress was the 1908 webbing pattern.

Weapons

The regiment was armed with the S.M.L.E. rifle (95 C) and bayonet (95 f), while officers carried the rifle-pattern sword (91 C).

Historical Note

The 83rd and 86th regiments were raised in September 1793 and November 1793 respectively. They amalgamated in 1881 to form the 1st and 2nd Battalions the Royal Irish Rifles. The title was changed to Royal Ulster Rifles in 1920, and in 1948 they were reduced to one battalion and titled 1st Battalion Royal Ulster Rifles (83rd and 86th). On 1 July 1968 the regiment amalgamated with the Royal Inniskilling Fusiliers and the Royal Irish Fusiliers to form the Royal Irish Rangers. The badge is a harp surmounted by a crown, under which is a scroll with the title 'Royal Irish Rangers'.

78. Field Marshal Earl Kitchener of Khartoum, 1915

Head Dress

The home-service-pattern forage cap was made of khaki cloth 3¼ in. deep with 3 cloth welts. A scarlet band 1¾ in. wide encircled the cap between the 2 lower welts. The chinstrap was of black patent leather, attached to the cap by 2 buttons behind the corners of the peak. The peak was set at an angle of 45 degrees and measured 2 in. deep in the centre. It was embroidered all round the edge with oakleaf-pattern wire embroidery. The badge was the design of an open-topped wreath of laurels surmounted by the Royal Crest. In the centre of the wreath were crossed batons for a Field Marshal. Other ranks of General Officers had crossed sword and baton.

Uniform

The tunic was of khaki drab material with plain cuffs and a lapelled collar. The collar was ornamented with gorget patches in scarlet cloth with a central line of oakleaf embroidery in gold for a Field Marshal. The tunic fastened down the front with 4 buttons, which bore the design of crossed batons and a crown within a laurel wreath. There were 4 pockets, one on each breast and one on each hip below the waist. The breast pockets had a box pleat and fastened with a flap and small button. At the waist were expanding pockets, the flap fastening with a button. There was a central vent at the back to the waist. Breeches of whipcord were worn with brown boots.

Accoutrements

A Sam Browne belt in brown leather was worn, with a cross strap passing over the right shoulder and fastening on the left side. The sword frog was attached to the left side. All fittings on the belt were brass.

Weapon

When carried in full dress, the sword was the General Officer's pattern (90 B).

Historical Note

Horatio Herbert Kitchener was born in 1850 and had a distinguished military career. In 1914 he was Secretary of State for War. He died when H.M.S. *Hampshire* sank in the North Sea *en route* for Russia in 1916. He had the following orders and decorations: K.G., K.P., G.C.B., O.M., G.S.C.I., G.C.M.G., G.C.I.E. These were Knight of the Garter, Knight of St Patrick, Member of Order of Merit, Knight Grand Commander of Star of India, Knight Grand Cross of St Michael and St George, Knight Grand Commander of Indian Empire. In the illustration is shown the famous recruiting poster bearing the bust of Kitchener which was designed and painted by Alfred Leete.

79. Lancashire Fusiliers (20th). Privates, 1915

Head Dress

The helmet worn was the foreign-service Wolseley pattern. The body was in cork covered in khaki drill cloth, with 6 seams. Peaks measured 3 in. wide at the front, 4 in. at the back and 2 in. at the sides. A khaki-covered zinc button fitted into a ventilation collet at the top. The chinstrap was in brown leather (black for rifle regiments). The helmet was bound around the headband with a khaki pugree. The left side of the helmet on the pugree was decorated with a scarlet patch bearing in white embroidery a Fusilier grenade above the letters L.F. denoting Lancashire Fusiliers.

Uniform

The tunic was the home-service pattern in khaki serge with a stand-and-fall collar and 4 pockets, 2 below the waist and 1 on each breast. The tunic fastened with 5 general-service-pattern buttons. Shoulder straps in khaki cloth bore the regimental title of L.F. and a grenade in brass. On each shoulder below the straps were 2 reinforced panels sewn to the tunic. There were 2 vents at the back. Trousers were also in khaki serge and worn with puttees and black boots.

Accoutrements

Other ranks of the Lancashire Fusiliers in 1915 still had the 1903 leather equipment of a 5-pouch bandolier over the left shoulder and a waist-belt also in brown leather with 2 pouches at each side. On the left hip was the bayonet frog. A water-bottle and haversack were carried. On the back was a pack and rolled blanket.

Weapons

Contemporary photographs of the regiment before the landings at Gallipoli show the rifle carried as being the Lee-Enfield (95 B) with 1888-pattern bayonet (95 e).

Historical Note

At the landings in the Dardanelles the 1st Battalion the Lancashire Fusiliers nearly equalled the Army record of the most Victoria Crosses won in a single action. This distinction was held by the 24th Foot (later South Wales Borderers and now 1st Battalion The Royal Regiment of Wales). The Lancashire

Fusiliers won 6 'before breakfast' during the landings. The recipients were Captain Richard Raymond Willis, Sergeant Alfred Richards, Private William Keneally, Captain (temporary Major) Cuthbert Bromley, Sergeant Frank Edward Stubbs and Corporal John Grimshaw. All were selected by their comrades in the regiment for their gallantry in the landings at W beach on 25 April 1915.

80. East Surrey Regiment (31st and 70th). Sergeant and Private, 1917

Head Dress

The cap worn in the illustration was similar in shape to the forage cap, but had a soft peak, which had as stiffening many lines of stitching. The chinstrap was of brown leather held at either side of the peak with a small general-service-pattern button. Besides the forage cap the other cap worn was called the 'Gor-blimey' and was a soft cap with folding earflaps. The soft cap with the unstiffened peak was issued in 1917. The 'Gor-blimey' was worn in the early part of the First World War.

Uniform

The tunic was in khaki serge cloth and had a stand-and-fall collar. It fastened with 5 general-service-pattern buttons. The back of the skirts had 2 vents. There were 4 pockets, one on each breast with a pocket flap and small button and one each side below the waist flap and button. Shoulder straps were khaki, with the regimental title in brass. At each shoulder was a re-inforced patch of khaki cloth sewn to the tunic. Trousers were of the same material and worn with khaki puttees and black boots.

Accoutrements

Equipment worn was the 1908 web pattern. This consisted of a waist-belt with brass buckles and 2 cross straps. On each side on the belt was a set of 5 ammunition pouches, the bottom 3 on the left side fastening with a small strap and stud, the rest with a flap and stud. On the back was worn the large pack, and at each side the water-bottle and small pack. An entrenching tool was carried in a web holder in the small of the back and the D-shaped mess-tin carried below the large pack. On the belt was a bayonet frog which had a fitment to carry the handle of the entrenching tool. The gas mask was carried either on the chest or slung on the left side.

Weapons

The regiment were armed with the S.M.L.E. rifle (95 C) and bayonet (95 g).

Historical Note

Gas masks or respirators were first issued in May 1915, but when gas was first used the troops were told to soak their handkerchiefs in a solution of water and boracic acid and tie this across their mouths. Various pat-terns of respirator were issued to the troops, but by 1917 a standard gas mask was in use. In the illustration the private on the right has on his left

sleeve 2 wound stripes. The wound stripe was authorised by Army Order 249 of 1916. They were of gold Russia braid, 2 in. in length and sewn per-pendicularly on the sleeve of the jacket. If more than one wound the stripes were $\frac{1}{2}$ in. apart. Later these stripes were also made in metal. Wound stripes were revived in the Second World War by Army Order 19 of 1944 for wear on battle dress and service dress.

81. Seaforth Highlanders (Ross-shire Buffs, The Duke of Albany's) (72nd and 78th). R.S.M. and Private, 1917

Head Dress

A khaki bonnet resembling the Bal-moral bonnet is shown, with a khaki worsted pom-pom on the top. The badge worn on the left side showed a stag's head with a scroll beneath carrying the motto *Cuidich'n Righ*.

Uniform

The tunic was of khaki serge cloth cut on the lines of a doublet, the bot-tom edge being rounded and cut away at the front. The tunic had a stand-and-fall collar and fastened by means of 5 general-service-pattern buttons. Buttons were in brass and bore the design of the Royal Coat of Arms in relief. There were 4 pockets on the tunic, 1 on each breast and 1 each side below the waist, the top 2 having flaps and buttons, the others having flaps only and being inside pockets. On each shoulder was a strap with the regimental designation in brass. Below the straps were 2 reinforced panels of khaki cloth. The kilt of the Mackenzie tartan was worn on active service with the addition of a khaki apron back and front, the front part having a flapped pocket in place of the sporran. Socks were khaki and worn with red garter tabs and puttees. Ordinary infantry tunics were also worn.

Accoutrements

The equipment worn was the 1908-pattern web. This was the first equipment to be fitted together in one piece. Everything was an integral part of the whole and could be taken off and put on complete. The equipment was a wide web belt with a brass buckle at the front and 2 at the back with short straps. There were 2 shoulder braces and 2 sets of 5 pouches fitted each side at the front to the belt. The rest of the equipment included small pack, water-bottle and carrier, large pack, mess-tin in cover, bayonet frog with attachment for entrenching-tool handle, entrenching-tool head cover and gas mask in case. The R.S.M. wore on the left side of the waist-belt a revolver in a leather holster.

Weapons

The men were armed with the S.M.L.E. rifle (95 C) and long bayonet (95 g). The R.S.M. carried the Webley Mk V or VI (Revolvers, Appendix 2).

82. Royal Artillery. Gunners, 1918

Head Dress

The head dress worn was the steel helmet introduced into the British Army in 1916. It was painted khaki and had an adjustable chinstrap and lining.

Uniform

The tunic was the standard pattern with a stand-and-fall collar and with 2 pockets, one on each breast, with a flap and small button. Below the waist at each side was a pocket with flap fastening with a button. The shoulder straps were ornamented with the initials in brass of R.H.A. (Royal Horse Artillery) or R.F.A. (Royal Field Artillery) or R.G.A. (Royal Garrison Artillery) or R.A. (Royal Artillery) according to which part of the regiment the gunner belonged. R.A. on the shoulder straps were worn only by Ammunition Columns and the Artillery Clerks' section. The Royal Garrison Artillery were dressed as dismounted men, the others as mounted men. Trousers with puttees were worn, the puttees wound from the knee to the boot and not as worn in the Infantry. The gunner on the left of the illustration is wearing a leather shell carrier, with 4 shells, 2 each side. Because of the weight of some of the shells, this was found a satisfactory method for carrying them.

Accoutrements

The normal equipment worn by the Royal Artillery was a 5-pouch brown leather bandolier. Gas masks were carried in a pack on the chest.

Weapons

As personal weapons the men used the S.M.L.E. rifle (95 C).

Historical Note

The illustration is taken from the figures on the Royal Artillery War Memorial at Hyde Park Corner, London.

83. Irish Guards. Guardsmen, 1934

Head Dress

The head dress worn was the regulation bearskin cap about 10 in. high and made of black bear. The fur was shaped on a wicker frame. A hair plume in St Patrick's blue was worn on the right side of the cap. The chinchain was of interlocking brass rings tapered in size and backed with black leather.

Uniform

The tunic was in scarlet cloth with blue collar, cuffs and shoulder straps. Top of the collar, cuffs and leading edge of the tunic were piped in white cloth. The collar was decorated each side with a shamrock leaf in white embroidery. Shoulder straps had on them the star of the Order of St Patrick, the centre part formed by a small regimental-pattern button. Sergeants and bandsmen had different badges on shoulder straps. The tunic fastened by 10 buttons grouped 4, 4 and 2. Buttons were brass with the design of the harp and crown. Cuffs were round and had a slashed panel in blue. The panel was decorated with 4 buttons and white button loops in the centre of the panel. Skirts at the back were ornamented with 2 slashed panels with 4 buttons and button loops on each and piped in blue with a central piping of white between. There were 2 regimental-pattern buttons at the waist above the panels. Trousers were of blue cloth, with a scarlet welt down the outside seam of each leg.

Accoutrements

Equipment at this time was of the Slade Wallace pattern, but not complete. Only the waist-belt, bayonet frog and 2 cross braces were worn. The belt was fastened by a regimental-pattern locket, which was in brass and was the star of the Order of St Patrick circumscribed 'Irish Guards'. On the back was the folded Atholl grey greatcoat, with in the centre on the strap the badge of the Order of St Patrick. Braces and folded greatcoat were worn for Guard Mounting and other ceremonies.

Weapons

The rifle carried was the S.M.L.E. (95 E) and 1907 bayonet (95 g).

84. 4th Battalion 1st Punjab Regiment. Subadar and Sepoy, 1934

Head Dress

The head dress was the lungi of yellow cloth with lines of gold and blue. The sepoy in service dress wore a khaki lungi with a small red fringe at the top.

Uniform

The subadar in full dress wore a scarlet tunic with collar, cuffs and shoulder straps of the face colour, which in this case was grass green. Down the front were 8 buttons of regimental pattern: gilt convex with the image of a distorted dragon wearing the Imperial Crown. Cuffs were pointed and edged round the top with a band of gold lace. Piping down the leading edge was grass green, matching that on the back of the skirts. Shoulder straps were grass green and edged in gold lace, with the ranking for a subadar of 2 stars. Around the waist was worn a crimson netted sash knotting on the left side and ending in tassels and fringes. The sepoy wore a khaki service dress blouse with 2 patch pockets on the breast and with a fly-front fastening. Shoulder straps were khaki with the regimental title in brass. Trousers and puttees were khaki. In full dress trousers were blue with a $\frac{1}{4}$-in. welt in scarlet cloth down the outer seam. Blue puttees were worn, but white spats were permitted.

Accoutrements

The subadar wore a web waist-belt under the tunic with 2 sword slings, one long and one short, of gold lace with a scarlet train in the centre and backed with morocco leather. Other ranks wore a plain brown leather belt in parade order, replaced by the 1908-pattern webbing equipment when in full marching order.

Weapons

Subadars and officers carried a nickel-plated Infantry-pattern sword with the Imperial cipher on the guard in a nickel-plated scabbard (91 B). Rank and file were armed with the S.M.L.E. rifle (95 C)

Historical Note

The regiment's pre-1903 title was the 1st Brahman Infantry, which changed in 1903 to the 1st Brahmans. During the First World War they were the 1st Battalion 1st Brahmans, and in 1922 became the 4th Battalion 1st Punjab Regiment.

85. The Leicestershire Regiment (17th). R.S.M. and Private, 1937

Head Dress

The head dress worn was the khaki cloth-covered Wolseley pattern helmet. The cork body was covered in khaki drill and bound all round in the same material. The covering had 6 seams. A rim projected 3 in. to the front, 4 in. at the back and 2 in. at the sides. The helmet top carried a khaki drill covered zinc button screwed into a collet which acted as a ventilator. The helmet was bound around the headband with a khaki pugree. The chinstrap, $\frac{3}{4}$ in. wide, was of brown or black leather. Patches or flashes were allowed to be worn on the side of the helmet on the pugree. Dress Regulations (India) 1931 stated that 'such permission extends to British Units while serving within Indian limits or on the Indian establishment'. Dress Regulations for the Army 1934 stated: 'No badges, hackles or ornaments of any description, except regimental patches, may be worn with the khaki helmet, except by the Brigade of Guards, who wear regimental-pattern plumes and pagri badges, by the Royal Fusiliers, who wear a white plume, the Black Watch, who wear a red hackle, the Duke of Cornwall's Light Infantry, who wear red feathers, the Lancashire Fusiliers, who wear a yellow hackle, the Royal Inniskilling Fusiliers, who wear a grey plume, and the Royal Berkshire Regiment, who wear a strip of red cloth 1¼ in. wide on the right side of the helmet. Regimental patches will be worn on the left side of the khaki helmet.'

Uniform

Jacket and shorts were of khaki drill cloth. The jacket was cut full at the chest and fastened down the front with 5 brass buttons. The collar was of the stand-and-fall pattern. Shoulder straps were also of khaki drill cloth. There were 2 vents at the back. Sleeves had pointed cuffs of the same material and colour. There were 2 pockets, one on each breast, with a box pleat in each and the flap fastened with a small brass button. Khaki drill cloth shorts were worn with hose and puttees. The R.S.M. had the usual badge of rank on the arm.

Accoutrements

The private wore the 1908-pattern webbing equipment with 2 sets of pouches on the front. The R.S.M. wore the Sam Browne belt with brace and sword frog.

Weapons

The R.S.M. carried the Infantry sword (91 B), and rank and file were armed with the S.M.L.E. rifle (95 C) and long bayonet 1907 pattern (95 g).

86. Royal Bombay Sappers and Miners. Drum Major and Drummer, 1937

Head Dress

A dark blue lungi with a yellow fringe hanging on the left side was worn by the Drum Major. Drummers wore the same type of head dress, but with the lungi tied around a kullah or small pointed cap which was in red cloth. Topping the kullah at the back of the lungi was a starched blue fan. A yellow fringe hung on the left side of the lungi.

Uniform

A long tunic of scarlet cloth finished just above the knees. Collar and cuffs were of blue cloth, the collar bound top and bottom in white tape and cuffs edged in white tape with a design of a crow's-foot knot at the point. The leading edge of the tunic was piped in blue. Shoulder straps were of red cloth and bore the regimental title in brass. The tunic fastened by means of 6 buttons of corps pattern down the front. Blue twisted body cords were worn by drummers and Drum Major. These fastened to the top button, looped under the right arm and shoulder strap, crossed the body and fastened to the left shoulder, ending in tassels and fringes. A thick black cloth waist-belt, fastened by a large rectangular brass plate, bore the corps badge and title. Trousers were of dark

194

blue cloth and had a wide scarlet stripe running down each outside seam. Dark blue puttees were worn.

Accoutrements

The Drum Major wore white gauntlet gloves and carried a staff of malacca, the top of which was decorated with the regimental honours and title. This decoration was in the form of a large silver grenade. The drummer wore a white buff leather drum sling over the right shoulder, terminating in a ring and thong on the left front. The drum had a hook on the top hoop to fit to the sling. The body of the drum was in brass and sometimes decorated. The hoops were edged in blue at the top and red at the bottom. A white wavy line divided the blue central stripe. The Corps also had pipers.

Historical Note

The Bombay Sappers and Miners were raised in 1820, although a company of Pioneer Lascars had existed in the Bombay Forces since 1777. The title 'Royal' was bestowed on the Corps in 1920 as a reward for services during the First World War.

87. The Queen's Royal Regiment (West Surrey) (2nd). Privates, 1938

Head Dress

The helmet was made of manganese steel about 12 in. from side to side and 14 in. from front to back. Around the domed top was a rim 1½ in. wide. The helmet was painted olive drab and had an elasticised chinstrap covered in drab green cloth. Helmet transfers decorated the head dress.

Uniform

The blouse was of khaki serge with a stand-and-fall collar and with cuffs that fastened with a button. The blouse buttoned down the front with 4 plastic khaki buttons hidden from view by a fly. Shoulder straps of khaki serge cloth had a plastic button at the top. The upper arms were decorated, below the shoulder straps, with the regimental title flash. The blouse fastened at the waist with a strap and buckle. There were patch pockets on either breast, the flap fastening with a khaki button. Trousers, also of khaki serge, had a large pocket on the left leg above the knee. Another pocket just below the waist on the right leg carried field service dressing. At the ankle a button fastening enabled the 6-in.-high anklets of webbing to be worn correctly. Anklets were of the same material as the webbing equipment, fastening with 2 straps and brass buckles.

Accoutrements

The equipment was the 1937 W.E. (web equipment). This consisted of a waist-belt, 2 braces with 2 attachment braces, water-bottle with carrier, haversack with left and right shoulder strap, 2 ammunition pouches, bayonet frog and large pack. A gas mask in case was also worn on the chest.

Weapons

The rifle carried was the S.M.L.E. (95 C) with long bayonet (95 g), although the new No. 4 Lee-Enfield rifle and spike bayonet was being introduced. The other private is holding a Bren gun (96 d).

Historical Note

Although battle dress was issued on trial in 1937 and issued in 1938 to the newly conscripted militia, it was not mentioned in Army Council Instructions until 1940 under the heading A.C.I. 306.

88/89. The Middlesex Regiment (Duke of Cambridge's Own) 8th Battalion (57th and 77th). Vickers Machine-gun Demonstration Section, 1939

Head Dress

In service dress the Army wore the steel helmet. The helmet had been introduced in 1916, replacing the khaki forage cap for active service. It was made of steel with a removable liner and head band. The chinstrap was elasticised webbing. The helmet of 1939 differed very little from the original pattern and measured 12½ in. from side to side and 14 in. from front to back. Around the domed top was a 1½-in. rim. It was painted olive green drab, the same colour as the equipment. On the left side was a regimental transfer. In the case of the Middlesex Regiment this was a lozenge halved vertically, with the left side yellow (the regimental facing colour) and the right side red.

Uniform

The uniform was as that worn during the First World War, although battle dress had been introduced for the Regular Army and many Territorial Army battalions by this date. The jacket was single-breasted with a stand-and-fall collar and buttoning down the front with 5 general-service buttons. Collars were ornamented with the regimental collar badge in brass and white metal. The Prince of Wales' feathers and motto (in white metal) above the coronet and cipher 'G' of H.R.H. the late Duke of Cambridge interlaced and reversed (in brass). Below the cipher was a scroll with the battle honour AL-BUHERA. The whole was surrounded by a laurel wreath, the scroll with the battle honour at the base. Shoulder straps were held at the top with a small brass general-service-pattern button. On the straps, in brass and curved, was the word 'Middlesex'. The jacket had 2 patch pockets with flaps, 1 on each breast, and 2 reinforced patches at the shoulders. The back of the jacket was plain, with 2 small vents at the bottom of the back seams. Ranking for non-commissioned officers was in chevron tape, as were the long-service stripes. Trousers were in the same material and the same colour and worn with khaki puttees wound from bottom to top and with the trousers folded over slightly. Boots were black.

Accoutrements

Equipment was the 1908-pattern webbing. It was the first set of equipment ever adopted by the British

Army that fitted as one unit and could be taken off or put on together. Previously water-bottle and haversack had separate straps, but in the 1908-pattern equipment the water-bottle and haversack attached to the ends of the cross straps. The bayonet frog fitted to the belt on the left side, the belt having a brass buckle at the front and 2 brass buckles and straps at the back. All buckles were of brass. The 2 shoulder straps buckled to the 2 sets of 5 pouches on the belt either side at the front and passed over the shoulders, crossed at the back and buckled there to smaller buckles. The haversack was worn on the left side and the water-bottle on the right, both attached to the ends of the braces. The large pack was worn on the back and an entrenching-tool cover at the back below the belt. The D-shaped mess-tin in a khaki canvas cover was carried strapped to the large pack or worn where the braces crossed when the pack was not worn.

The gas mask was carried in a canvas case worn around the neck and tied around the body with a cord. In the illustration the demonstration section wore white numbers on black canvas on the gas-mask case.

Weapons

The men were armed with the Short Lee-Enfield Mk 3 (95 C) with 1907-pattern bayonet (95 g). The machine-gun in service was the Vickers 0·303 medium (96 b).

Historical Note

At this time machine-guns were regimented, and certain line regiments were selected to become machine-gun battalions. Among those so designated were the Northumberland Fusiliers (5th), The Cheshire Regiment (22nd), Middlesex Regiment (57th and 77th), The Manchester Regiment (63rd and 96th) and the Argyll and Sutherland Highlanders (91st and 93rd).

APPENDIX 1

Plate 90

A. *Basket hilted Broadsword or Claymore, 1831.* This traditional weapon of Scottish regiments other than the Cameronians was authorised for the first time in Dress Regulations of 1831. The popular name 'claymore' is taken from the large two-handed broadsword, the Claidheamh Mor, used by the early Scots.

Regulations call for the hilt to be cast in malleable iron, although present-day weapons are either of sheet steel or cast gilding metal. The hilt is lined with white buckskin, covered in red superfine cloth, edged with blue silk. The grip is of wood covered with fish-skin and bound with three silver wires. At the pommel it is dressed with a crimson silk fringe.

When in undress uniform the basket hilt was removed, and in its place was fitted a crosshilt of regimental pattern as follows:

Left-hand side, top to bottom.

> Royal Scots
> Royal Scots Fusiliers and, with languets, Highland Light Infantry
> Seaforth Highlanders, Cameron Highlanders and the Argyll and Sutherland Highlanders

Right-hand side, top to bottom.

> King's Own Scottish Borderers
> Black Watch and Gordon Highlanders
> Band Sergeants of Scottish Regiments

B. *General Officer's Scimitar, 1831 Pattern* (as amended). Introduced for wear by General Officers by His Grace the Duke of Wellington when Commander-in-Chief, this sword is in current use. The sword has a slightly curved blade $32\frac{1}{2}$ in. in length, from shoulder to point; originally carried in a black leather scabbard with gilt mounts for wear at levées, drawing-rooms and in evening dress and in a brass scabbard for wear in the field, it is now invariably carried in a nickel-plated scabbard.

The grip is of gilt brass, faced with two ivory scales decorated with rosettes, and the crossguard is cast in brass and gilded. In the centre it bears the rank badge.

C. *Royal Scots Fusiliers Regimental Pattern, c. 1870.* In the latter part of the nineteenth century officers of the Royal Scots Fusiliers carried, by custom rather than regulation, their own regimental-pattern sword. This was a development of the 1822-pattern sword for Infantry officers, and in the bars of the gilt brass guard was arranged a bursting grenade flanked by two thistles, the whole encircled by a scroll bearing the regimental title and the motto *Nemo me impune lacessit*.

D. *Royal Engineers, 1856 Pattern.* The hilt of this sword was identical to that worn by Heavy Cavalry officers, except that the hilt was in gunmetal instead of steel. It was decorated with an elaborate scrolled pattern, and the pommel and backpiece were deeply chequered.

The blade was slightly curved and about 32 in. long, terminating in a spear point. It was carried in a dark brown leather scabbard fitted with three gun-metal mounts, the top two fitted with rings for sling suspension.

E. *Pioneer's Hanger, 1856 Pattern.* This sword had a blade 22½ in. in length, the top 16 in. of the back edge being a cross-cut saw, the remainder sharpened to an axe edge. The blade section tapered in wedge shape to its normal cutting edge. It had a knuckle bow of brass, and the grip was formed by fitting brass scales to an extension of the blade. It was carried in a black leather scabbard with a brass chape and top mount fitted with a stud for frog suspension.

Originally designed for use in the construction of defence works and for the clearing of timber to give improved fields of fire, it was withdrawn in 1903, conceivably because it was considered a barbarous weapon.

F. *Royal Artillery, 1855 Pattern.* Although carried by Royal Horse Artillery officers from 1833, this sword was first prescribed for officers of Artillery Battalions in Dress Regulations of 1855. It is of the same pattern as the Light Cavalry sword of 1822, except that by custom the pommel is stepped instead of being chequered. The blade is slightly curved and 35½ in. from shoulder to point, terminating in a spear point. It is carried in a nickel-plated steel scabbard with two suspension rings approximately 8 in. apart.

G. *Bandsman's Sword, 1895 Pattern.* Officially designated 'Sword, Drummer's Mark II and Bugler's, Line Regiments, brass with buff piece', this sword was introduced into the Army in 1895 with a companion weapon 'Sword, Bugler's, Mark II and Band, Rifle Regiments, iron hilt with buff piece'. Both were of the same design.

The overall length of the weapon was nearly 19 in. and the blade was 13¼ in. long. The hilt was cast in three parts, crossguard, grip and top cap to cover the securing nut on the end of the tang. It was carried in a black leather scabbard, fitted with a chape and top mount, the metal of the scabbard mounts matching that of the grip.

Plate 91

A. and B. *Infantry Officers' Swords*. Dress Regulations of 1822 introduced for the first time a new sword that embodied in the design of the hilt the cipher of His Majesty the King. The regulations stated:

Gilt half-basket with G iv R inserted in the outward bars and lined with black patent leather. Grip of black fish-skin bound with three gilt wires. The blade 32½ in. in length, with round back terminating to a shampre within 9 in. of the point and very little curved. Scabbard black with gilt mountings, steel in the field. To be carried by Garrison Staff, Royal Military Asylum, Provost Marshal, Medical, Commisariat, Paymaster, Judge Advocate, Foot Guards and Infantry of the Line (A).

In 1834 field officers had adopted a brass scabbard, and in 1846 the rounded back of the blade was dropped in favour of the 'Wilkinson' pattern with a strong flat back and an even taper from the cutting edge to give the cross-section a wedge shape.

The guard, of three bars with an oval cartouche in the outward two, was known as of 'Gothic pattern'; in the cartouche was carried the cipher of the ruling monarch, and these were: VR (Victoria Regina); VRI (Victoria Regina, Imperatrix. Indian Army only); ER (Edwardus Rex. Medical Corps only); GvR (Medical Corps only).

The sword was carried by Infantry until the introduction in 1892 of the new pattern, with a steel guard bearing the Royal cipher on the face (B). Royal Army Medical Corps officers continued to carry the pattern until varied by Dress Regulations of 1934.

Staff Officers carried the sword from 1834 until the latter part of the nineteenth century with the cartouche carrying the rank badge of a Major-General. Regiments of Foot Guards, from 1855, carried their regimental emblem in lieu of the cipher in the cartouche, and later changed from a brass handguard to one of polished steel (G).

Rifle Regiments carried this pattern in polished steel with the cartouche badged with the crown and bugle-horn stringed (C). The Cameronians (Scottish Rifles) had in the cartouche the five-pointed star surrounded by a plain Garter, all surrounded by a wreath of thistles (H), and the Honourable East India Company carried the brass hilt, incorporating their own badge in the cartouche (E).

The Volunteer Regiment, Queen Victoria's Rifles, had their own pattern, carrying in the cartouche the image of St George and the Dragon (D).

The 1892 pattern, amended in 1895 by lapping the inside of the guard to prevent damage to the uniform by rubbing, has been carried by all Infantry other than Guards and Rifle Regiments. It is also carried by officers of Royal Engineers, Royal Corps of Signals, Royal Army Ordnance Corps, Royal

Electrical and Mechanical Engineers, Royal Army Pay Corps, Royal Army Educational Corps and Royal Pioneer Corps.

MEDALS

Plate 92

A. *The Victoria Cross.* The Victoria Cross was instituted by Queen Victoria by the Royal Warrant of 29 January 1856, to be awarded to officers and other ranks 'who have performed some single act of Valour or devotion to their country'.

The design is of a Maltese Cross in bronze $1\frac{1}{2}$ in. across. In the centre is a lion passant gardant upon a crown with a scroll underneath bearing the words FOR VALOUR. The cross is suspended by a bronze bar decorated with laurel leaves and a link in the shape of a V.

The reverse of the cross has a raised edge and a circle in which is engraved the date of the action for which the Cross has been awarded. The recipient's name appears on the back of the bar.

At the first distribution by Queen Victoria in Hyde Park sixty-two Victoria Crosses were awarded.

The ribbon was crimson for the Army and blue for the Navy until the First World War, when crimson was adopted for all services.

B. and **C.** *The Crimea Medal.* The obverse of this medal shows the 'young' head of Queen Victoria with the inscription VICTORIA REGINA round the outer edge and the date 1854 at the bottom.

The reverse shows a Roman soldier holding a sword and shield crowned with a wreath of laurels by a winged figure representing Victory. To the left is the word CRIMEA written vertically.

The suspender is of a foliage design. Five bars were awarded of an oakleaf design bearing the names of the battles in which the recipient took part. The battles were: ALMA; BALAKLAVA; INKERMAN; SEBASTOPOL; AZOFF. The last of these was awarded to Naval personnel who took part in the operations in the Sea of Azoff. The ribbon is light blue with yellow edges.

C. and **D.** *The Indian Mutiny Medal.* The obverse of this medal is identical to that of the Crimea medal except that the date 1854 has been omitted.

The reverse shows a figure of Britannia holding a laurel wreath in her outstretched right hand and with a Union shield on her left arm. The British lion is shown in the background. The top edge of the medal bears the word INDIA. In the exergue at the base of the medal are the dates 1857–1858.

Five bars were awarded for operations during the Mutiny; they had fish-tailed ends and were separated from each other by small rosettes. The bars bear the following inscriptions, DELHI; LUCKNOW; RELIEF OF LUCKNOW; DEFENCE OF LUCKNOW; CENTRAL INDIA. This was the last medal issued by the Honourable East India Company. The ribbon is white with two ¼-in. red stripes.

F. and **G.** *Queen's South Africa Medal.* The obverse of this medal bears the crowned and veiled head of Queen Victoria, with the inscription *Victoria Regina et Imperatrix* around the outer edge.

The reverse shows the standing figure of Britannia holding a laurel wreath in her outstretched right hand and a flag in the crook of her left arm. In the background are soldiers in line of march and two ships. On the ground behind Britannia is a Union shield and a trident. The top edge of the medal bears the words SOUTH AFRICA.

Twenty-six bars were issued: CAPE COLONY; NATAL; RHODESIA; RELIEF OF MAFEKING; DEFENCE OF KIMBERLEY; TALANA; ELANDSLAAGTE; DEFENCE OF LADYSMITH; BELMONT; MODDER RIVER; TUGELA HEIGHTS; RELIEF OF KIMBERLEY; PAARDEBERG; ORANGE FREE STATE; RELIEF OF LADYSMITH; DRIEFONTEIN; WEPENER; DEFENCE OF MAFEKING; TRANSVAAL; JOHANNESBURG; LAINGS NEK; DIAMOND HILL; WITTERBERGEN; BELFAST; SOUTH AFRICA 1901; SOUTH AFRICA 1902.

The ribbon is red with two blue stripes and a thick orange stripe in the centre.

E. and **F.** *The Third China War Medal 1900.* The obverse of this medal is identical to that of the Queen's South Africa Medal.

The reverse shows a large trophy of arms with a shield bearing the Royal Arms, all under a palm tree. On the top edge is the inscription *Armis Exposcere Pacem.* In the exergue is the word CHINA and the date 1900.

Three bars were issued to those troops entitled. They were: TAKU FORTS; DEFENCE OF LEGATIONS; RELIEF OF PEKIN.

The ribbon was crimson with yellow edges.

H. *The Military Cross.* The Military Cross was instituted by the Royal Warrant dated 31 December 1914. Recipients must be serving members of the Army, and must be of warrant or commissioned rank.

The Cross is of silver ornamented at the end of each arm with the Imperial Crown. In the centre is the Royal Cipher G.R. The clasp is of plain silver with a slot for the ribbon. The ribbon is white with a centre stripe of purple.

SOME OF THE MORE NOTABLE CAMPAIGN MEDALS AWARDED DURING THE PERIOD
1850–1945

Queen Victoria

New Zealand/India General Service 1854–95/South Africa 1850–53/ Crimea/ Baltic/Indian Mutiny/China 1857–60/Canada General Service 1866–70/ Abyssinia/Ashantee 1873–74/South Africa 1877–79/Afghanistan/Cape of Good Hope General Service/Egypt/North West Canada/East and West Africa/British South Africa Company Medals for Matabeleland, Rhodesia and Mashonaland/Ashanti Star/India General Service 1895/Central Africa/ Sudan/East and Central Africa/Royal Niger Company Medal/Queen's South Africa Medal 1899–1902/China 1900/Queen's Mediterranean.

King Edward VII

King's South Africa 1901–2/Tibet Medal/Natal Rebellion/Ashanti 1901/ Africa General Service 1902/India General Service 1908.

King George V

Africa General Service/India General Service/1914 Star/1914–15 Star/War Medal 1914–20/Mercantile Marine Medal 1914–18/Victory Medal/General Service Medal/Territorial Force War Medal 1914–19.

King George VI

India General Service 1936/General Service Medal/1939–45 Star/Atlantic Star/Air Crew Europe Star/Africa Star/Pacific Star/Burma Star/Italy Star/ France and Germany Star/Defence Medal/War Medal 1939–45.

Plate 93

SHAKO AND HELMET PLATES 1855–1914

With the authorisation of a new shako (sometimes called the second Albert Pattern) on 16 January 1855 a new plate was introduced for both officers and rank and file (A).

The plate for officers was a stamped gilt brass backplate surmounted by a crown. Pinned in the centre was in some cases a circle with the regimental title or motto, but in most cases the Garter belt with motto *Honi soit qui mal y pense*. In the centre of the circle or Garter on a black patent leather ground was the regimental number, or in some cases the number and authorised badge. Battle honours were borne on the plates by some regiments, and the scrolls with the names were invariably fitted to the top and bottom outer edges of the circle or Garter belt.

The other ranks' plate was of the same shape and size, being die-stamped in brass in one piece. The central part was the Garter belt and motto, within which was the regimental number pierced out (B). On 28 November 1860 another new pattern of shako was authorised. It is known as the quilted pattern by virtue of the way the cloth is attached to the body. The shako plate for both officers and other ranks was that worn by other ranks on the previous shako. The officers' pattern was in heavy gilt brass. Many varieties of both the above-mentioned plates can be found in numerous Militia and Volunteer units. Although of the same size and employing the star plate in most cases, these do not always follow the pattern worn by the Infantry of the Line. In 1869 a new pattern shako was authorised, and with it an entirely new pattern of plate (C). The officers' pattern plate consisted of 2 sprays of laurels surmounted by a crown and tied at the bottom with a ribbon. In the centre was a Garter belt with motto. In some cases this was replaced by a circle with the regimental title or motto. The normal pattern had inside this the pierced-out regimental number. Again in some instances use was made of an authorised regimental badge and the number. Honours were worn on the badge in some cases, and invariably these were placed below the Garter belt. The other ranks' plate followed the design of the officers' pattern, the number being pierced out in the centre. In 1878, with the introduction of the helmet to replace the shako, a new and larger plate was used. That for officers was a gilt 8-pointed star plate surmounted by a crown. In the centre was the Garter belt with motto *Honi soit qui mal y pense* decorated either side with a spray of laurels. In the centre of the Garter belt on a velvet ground was the regimental number or number and badge where authorised (D). The other ranks' plate was of the same basic design, but stamped in one piece, with the regimental number in the centre of the Garter belt.

In 1881, with the implementation of the Cardwell reform and the Stanley Committee findings involving the linking of battalions under a territorial regimental title, the numbers or numbers and badges gave way to the new territorial badge of the regiment (E and F).

The officers' plate was basically the same except that now inside the Garter belt was the territorial badge and beneath the Garter and pinned on the laurel spray was a silver scroll with the regimental title. The other ranks' plate changed the centre. Gone was the Garter belt and motto, and in its place was a circle with the new territorial title and the new badge within the circle.

The only other change made in helmet plates was in 1901 on the death of Queen Victoria, when the long-used Victorian crown gave way to the Tudor crown of King Edward VII (F).

The crown remained unaltered during the reign of George V. In 1914, when full dress went into store, an era was nearing its end. In 1918 it was not re-issued universally, but confined to ceremonial units such as bands.

SMALL ARMS IN BRITISH SERVICE

The latter half of the nineteenth century saw an ever-increasing efficiency in the rifles that were issued to the infantry of the British Army. Commencing the period with the smooth-bore percussion muskets, such as Lovell's pattern of 1842, the path of development led through the Minié rifle of 1851, the Enfield, pattern 1853, the Lancaster for Sappers and Miners, the Whitworth (never fully adopted and used only by the Rifle Brigade for a time), the Snider-Enfield, Martini-Henry, Martini-Metford, Martini-Enfield, Lee-Metford, Lee-Enfield, and now the semi-automatic self-loading rifles.

It is not possible in this volume to describe and discuss each and every one of these weapons, and we have chosen to illustrate and characterise the more popular of those in use during the period.

Plate 94

A. *The Enfield Rifle 1853 Pattern.* The 1853-pattern rifled musket was a muzzle-loading weapon, fired by the percussion system, i.e. a fulminate of mercury filled cap was positioned on a nipple at the closed end of the barrel, and on pressing the trigger a hammer descended with great force on to the cap, causing detonation; flame from this passed through a thin channel in the nipple and into the barrel, igniting the charge.

The Enfield, 4 ft. 7 in. long and weighing 8 lb. 14½ oz., fired a cylindro-conoidal bullet of 0·577 in. calibre of 530 grains of hardened lead. It had a muzzle velocity of 1,200 ft. per second and, like its predecessor the Minié, had a range of 1,000 yds., a great improvement on the Brunswick of 1838, which was sighted up to only 300 yds.

B. *The Snider-Enfield Rifle 1867.* The Enfield rifle was converted in 1867 into the Snider-Enfield by incorporating the breech invented by Jacob Snider of New York. Two inches of the butt end of the Enfield barrel were cut away to allow the cartridge and bullet, adapted by Colonel Boxer of Woolwich Arsenal, to be inserted with the thumb. The space behind the cartridge was then closed with an iron breech block, hinged to the right side of the barrel and bored centrally to accommodate a firing pin which, when the trigger was pressed, was driven by the hammer into the centrally placed detonating cap of the cartridge case.

Weights and dimensions of the weapon were unaltered by this conversion, and the bullet shape and size were identical with the muzzle-loading version.

C. *The Martini-Henry Rifle 1871.* This was a breech-loading central-fire weapon, with a calibre of 0·450 in. The breech was operated by lowering a lever beneath the small of the butt, which lowered the breech block. The cartridge, an adaptation of the Boxer, was then inserted with the thumb and the lever returned to its former position, thus closing the breech. The breech block was centrally pierced to accommodate the firing pin, which was driven forward on pulling the trigger by an internal hammer.

The Martini-Henry weighed 9 lb., was 4 ft. 1½ in. long and fired a hardened lead bullet of 480 grains with a muzzle velocity of 1,350 ft. per second. The weapon was sighted up to 1,000 yds.

Although in 1883 the Small Arms Committee had recommended a reduction of calibre to 0·401 in., and sealed patterns had been manufactured, together with 70,000 rifles, they were never introduced and were afterwards made into 0·45-in.-calibre Martini-Henry rifles, being designated Mark IV.

The Martini-Henry breech action continued in use with Metford and later Enfield barrels of 0·303-in. calibre for both carbines and rifles until *c.* 1910.

Plate 95

A. *The Lee-Metford Rifle 1887*. The Small Arms Committee, in 1887, decided to adopt a magazine rifle with a calibre reduced to 0·303 in. and the magazine and bolt action designed by an American, James P. Lee, of New York State. This action, modified and improved at the Royal Small Arms Factory at Enfield and married to the reduced-calibre barrel incorporating Metford's system of rifling, produced the Lee-Metford rifle.

It was 4 ft. 1¼ in. long and weighed 9½ lb., with a magazine holding 8 rounds. In the Mark II version this was increased to 10. The propellant was black gunpowder and the bullet solid hardened lead.

B. and **C.** *The Lee-Enfield Rifle 1895*. The introduction of cordite as a propellant charge sounded the death knell for the Metford system of rifling. Burning at a far higher temperature, it caused considerable erosion at the breech end of the barrel, and this fact, together with the unsuitability of the lead bullet, which was replaced with one having a cupro-nickel jacket, reduced the barrel life of the Lee-Metford to about 4,000 rounds.

A new barrel was therefore adopted with rifling developed by the Royal Small Arms factory at Enfield, and this weapon, practically indistinguishable externally from the Lee-Metford, came into service on 11 November 1895 as the Lee-Enfield Magazine Rifle, Mark I.

It was 4 ft. 1½ in. in length, and had a weight of 9 lb. 4 oz. It fired the standard service cartridge with a bullet of 0·303 calibre, and was sighted to fire up to 2,800 yds.

Following the Boer War came a demand for a shortened rifle suitable for both infantry and mounted troops. The opportunity was taken to redesign the Lee-Enfield rifle, at the same time incorporating improvements suggested by users with battle experience.

As a result, in December 1902, approval was given to the Short, Magazine, Lee-Enfield, Mark I, the universally known S.M.L.E. This was 5 in. shorter than its predecessor and was stocked to the muzzle. The breech incorporated charger guides, and the cartridges in metal chargers could be loaded in fives, involving two movements rather than ten, as with the single-loading magazine. The weight was reduced to 8 lb. 2½ oz. and it was sighted up to 2,800 yds.

There was a Mark II version, made by converting Lee-Metford Mark II and Lee-Enfield Mark I rifles, and in 1907 a Mark III was introduced, incorporating an improved charger guide, a blade foresight protected by 'wings' and a U backsight.

Quantity manufacture of a new pattern rifle, under trial in 1913, was curbed by outbreak of war in 1914. However, its characteristic of supreme accuracy made it an ideal weapon for snipers, and the Pattern 14 became the standard issue sniper rifle, fitted with telescopic sights.

The Ross Rifle (not illustrated). The Ross rifle was, prior to the first few months of the First World War, the standard arm of the Canadian Army. It differed from the Lee-Enfield in design of both bolt and magazine, the bolt being similar to that of the Mauser and the magazine enclosed in the stock and held in position by the trigger guard.

The Number 4 Rifle (not illustrated). The No. 4 Rifle Mark I was approved in 1939 for issue to the Army. Changes from the S.M.L.E. were in the method of sighting, there being a 'battle' aperture sight for a fixed range of 200 yds., which could be flipped into place.

Bolt and magazine were modified versions of the previous design, and barrel length was as before, though outside diameter was increased. The heavy block fore-end was replaced by a lighter version. Its weight was 9 lb. 1 oz. and it fired the standard service 0·303 in. ammunition, with a magazine capacity for 10 rounds.

BAYONETS IN GENERAL USE IN THE BRITISH ARMY 1850–1945

	Weight, lb. oz.		Blade length, in.
Enfield Rifle Pattern 1853 Long			
Socket bayonet P 53 1st model		11	17
P 53 2nd model		13½	17
P 59 Native Infantry		11	17
Enfield Rifle Pattern 1856 Short			
Sword bayonet P 56	1	12	23
Enfield Carbine, Artillery, etc.			
Sword bayonet P 53 and P 56	1	12	23

	Weight, lb. oz.		Blade length, in.
Lancaster Carbine			
Sword bayonet P 55	1	9	24
P 63	1	8	24
Snider Rifle Long			
As for Enfield Pattern 1853 long			
Snider Rifle Short			
As for Enfield Pattern 1856 short with the following			
Elcho sword bayonet P 1870	1	8	21
Snider Carbine, Artillery, etc.			
As for Enfield Artillery carbine with the following			
Sword bayonet P 75	1	4	18
Martini-Henry Pattern 1871			
Socket bayonet P 53 converted		11	17
P 76		15	21½
Sword bayonet P 56 converted	1	12	23
Elcho sword bayonet P 71	1	8	21
Sword bayonet P 86	1	4	18½
P 87 (*Experimental*)	1	4	18½
Martini-Henry Carbine, Artillery, etc.			
Sword bayonet P 79	1	10½	25¾
Martini, Metford and Enfield Carbine, Artillery, etc.			
Sword bayonet P 88 Mk II, III		16½	12¼
Martini-Enfield Rifle			
Socket bayonet P 95		15	21½
Lee-Metford Rifle			
Sword bayonet P 88 Mk I, II, III		16½	12¼
Lee-Enfield Rifle			
Sword bayonet P 88 Mk II, III		16½	12¼
Short Lee-Enfield			
Sword bayonet P 03		16½	12¼
P 07		18	17
Lee-Enfield No. 4 Rifle			
Spike bayonet No. 4 Mk I, II, II*, III		7	9

BRITISH ARMY MACHINE-GUNS

If we discount the Puckle gun, Patent No. 418 of 1718, for 'a portable gun or machine called a Defence which can be so quickly loaden as renders it next to impossible to carry any ship by boarding', then the first machine-gun of interest to the British Army was the Gatling. This was the first practical design of a continuous-fire weapon, and was invented in 1862 by Dr Richard Gatling, an American. Any number of from four to ten barrels were arranged to rotate around a central axis, each barrel being equipped with its own lock. Cartridges fell from a container above the gun, by gravity, each one entering the barrel, then located in the top position. By turning a crank the barrels moved around the axis, and as each reached the lowest position it fired, and as it moved on, the empty cartridge case was ejected.

The whole barrel assemblage of the Gatling was encased in a water-filled jacket, and under ideal conditions the weapon could maintain a volume of about 300 shots per minute. Naturally, with this new weapon, there were drawbacks: first, its size and weight, and secondly, due to faulty cartridge cases it was liable to jam at exactly the wrong moment. However, it was used by the armies of America, China, Turkey, Egypt, Japan, Russia and Great Britain. It was adopted by the British Navy in 1871 and a short time later by the British Army, being used with excellent effect in the Zulu War of 1879.

The Nordenfeldt machine-gun was adopted by the British Army in 1884. This had a 0·45-in. calibre, fired the Boxer cartridge and was a three-barrelled gun with a cyclic rate of 350 rounds per minute. Almost free from jamming faults, it became a popular weapon in the British service.

The Gardner gun was another American invention. The final design had a single barrel and could fire either single shot or bursts. It was more portable than its predecessors and had a cyclic rate of about 120 shots per minute.

Hiram Maxim, a naturalised Briton of American birth, invented the first recoil-operated machine-gun, having realised that the kick from firing a service rifle could be utilised to operate the breech mechanism and reload the weapon for further use.

The Maxim gun breech mechanism was such that cartridges in a webbing belt passed continuously through the weapon, each being fed into the barrel by the energy of the previous cartridge and ejected after being fired by its own.

The Maxim, manufactured by Vickers in England, was used by most European armies. After the death of Sir Hiram Maxim in 1915 an improved version became known as the Vickers gun.

The Hotchkiss gun, another American product, operated by its own power, in this case by an escape of the propellant gases. It had a rate of approximately 600 rounds per minute, which compared with the Maxim, but it tended to overheat. Whereas, the overheat problem was met in the Maxim or Vickers with a water jacket, in the Hotchkiss it was countered by concentric fins around the barrel. In British service it was used in the 1-pounder variety by the Navy and in 0·303 calibre by the Cavalry and Indian Army.

The Lewis gun, introduced into the British Army in 1915, was more of an automatic rifle than a machine-gun. A gas-operated weapon easily portable by one man and firing 0·303 ammunition in bursts of up to thirty rounds without overheating troubles, it was a favourite infantry weapon in the First World War. The ammunition was in drums fitting on the top of the breech, and these could be changed with ease. It was superseded in the late 1930s by the Bren, a name deriving from BRNO, the Czechoslovakian armament firm who invented it, and ENFIELD, the British Government arms works, where the 0·303 version was manufactured for British and Empire issue. This was once again a gas-operated weapon, and its use was more as an automatic rifle than a machine-gun.

Plate 96

A. *The Gatling Gun 1862*. The Gatling gun, as adopted by the British Army, was a six-barrel model, firing the Boxer 0·45-in. calibre cartridge. It had a barrel assembly and water jacket about 5 ft. 6 in. long and was mounted on a two-wheeled carriage similar to that of a field gun. Above the breech was a drum-shaped hopper or container which fed ammunition into the barrels by gravity. On the right side of the breech was the crank handle which when turned caused the barrel assembly to rotate on its axis and fire and reload the gun at a cyclic rate of about 300 rounds per minute. It was a clumsy weapon, and in action almost impossible to conceal.

B. *The Vickers Gun 1915*. The Vickers gun was a single-barrelled water-cooled recoil and gas-operated weapon based on the original patents of Sir Hiram Maxim. It fired standard service ammunition of 0·303 in. calibre, fed into the breech by means of canvas belts, each holding 250 rounds. The first round was fed by hand operation of a cocking leaver, then on pressing the trigger the round fired and its recoil and gas caused the breech block to move to the rear, ejecting the spent case and reloading the next cartridge.

The gun, which weighed 30 lb. with full water jacket, was mounted on a low tripod of 52 lb., with a full 360 degrees traverse. In practice, the gun was laid on a target and the tripod clamped, variation of line and elevation being applied by the gunner in order to increase the zone covered by the bullets.

Cyclic rate of fire was 500 rounds per minute. The gun was portable by two men, one carrying the weapon and the other the tripod. Two ammunition belts in metal boxes were carried by each of the other men in the detachment. It could also be mule packed, as for Indian service, each animal carrying a complete gun and 500 rounds.

C. *The Lewis Gun 1915*. The Lewis gun was a gas-operated light machine-gun, adopted by the British Army in 1915 to make up for loss in fire power resulting from tremendous casualties suffered by the highly trained regular army during the first few months of the First World War.

It was a single-barrelled, air-cooled weapon and fired the standard 0·303-in. calibre service ammunition. This was fed into the breech from flat drums, each containing 47 rounds. The gun had a barrel 26½ in. long and with its bipod mounting weighed 29 lb. It fired at a cyclic rate of 550 rounds per minute up to a sighted range of 1,900 yds.

An anti-aircraft mounting enabled the gun to be employed against low-flying aircraft, and also a Royal Flying Corps version of the weapon with a plain barrel without aluminium cooling fins was developed.

D. *The Bren Gun.* This weapon was first produced by the Skoda armament works at Brno in Czechoslovakia, and its name derives from that place and Enfield, where it was subsequently manufactured for British service. The British Army adopted it in 1935 as a light machine-gun for issue to the infantry on a scale of one per section. Subsequently it was issued to all arms of the service in varying quantities.

It fired the standard 0·303-in. service ammunition at a cyclic rate of between 450 and 550 rounds per minute, depending on the adjustment of the gas regulator, and was sighted for a tactical range of 600 yds., though its maximum exceeded 2,000 yds.

Ammunition was carried in magazines, each holding 28 rounds. The gun was normally served by two men, who between them were capable of carrying the gun on its bipod and about 30 magazines of ammunition. The weapon weighed 20 lb. and had a barrel length of 24 in.

There was an anti-aircraft tripod mounting for use against ground-attack aircraft, and also special mountings for use in Bren-gun carriers, jeeps and other wheeled vehicles. A naval mounting was also designed so that this versatile weapon could be employed on motor torpedo boats and air-sea rescue craft.

APPENDIX 2

The most important characteristic of the revolver is that it is essentially a defensive weapon for use at close quarters. With practice it can be fired extremely accurately, but in battle it is normally used hurriedly and at short range. A further distinction of the weapon is its ability to stop an adversary by the sheer shock effect of low muzzle velocity and a comparatively heavy bullet. A hit anywhere on the body by a revolver or automatic pistol of 0·45 in. calibre will knock a man down.

In 1835 Colonel Samuel Colt made his first hand gun with charges and bullets carried in a revolving cylinder and fired in turn through a fixed barrel, differing from the earlier 'pepperboxes', where the charges were loaded into a set of barrels that revolved about a central axis. In Britain Adams produced the first solid-framed double-action revolver; this could be fired either by trigger pressure to cock the hammer and rotate the cylinder or by cocking the hammer by hand and discharging by pulling the trigger. During the Crimean War most British officers carried either the Adams or the Colt, both percussion weapons.

The introduction of the cartridge hardly changed the appearance of the revolver; it was necessary only to fit the hammer with a firing pin and remove the nipples from the cylinder and bore the chambers through to accommodate the cartridges. The first revolver fitted with a device for automatic extraction of empty cases was the Enfield of 0·442 in. calibre – an unsatisfactory weapon and soon withdrawn.

By 1890 the gun trade had so contracted that revolver manufacture was almost entirely confined to three main manufacturers, Colt, Smith & Wesson and Thomas Webley of Birmingham, the latter two being the only makers of self-extracting weapons.

In August 1890 the Webley Mark I of 0·441 in. calibre was officially adopted by the British. This rugged weapon with a 4-in. barrel could withstand rough treatment yet still fire. In 1892 the calibre was changed to 0·455 in., and Army Regulations stated that provided an officer carried a pistol that would fire the Government ammunition there was no restriction as to make.

The Webley went through Marks I, II, III, IV, V and VI, and there were varieties, such as the Webley-Wilkinson, Webley-Pryse and Webley-Green (known as the W.G.). The Mark IV predominated in the Boer War and the Mark V in the First World War, although the Mark VI was produced in 1915.

In 1921 the Royal Small Arms Factory started to manufacture the Webley

Mark VI at Enfield under the name of Pistol, Revolver, Webley Mark VI, later changed to Pistol, Revolver No. 1, Mark VI.

In 1929 the Goverment decided to change the calibre of the service revolver to 0·38 in., and both Enfield and Webley produced these for the Army, the official designation being Pistol, Revolver, No. 2, Mark I. This was almost exactly a smaller version of the Webley Mark VI, the main difference being that with a smaller bullet it was not such a capable man-stopper.

APPENDIX 3

Equipment for the British soldier remained virtually unchanged from about 1790 until 1850. Minor variations apart, the style worn at the Battle of Waterloo reappeared during the Crimean War. The standard equipment of a soldier in full marching order from 1800 until 1850 consisted of 2 cross-belts, one holding the ammunition pouch and the other the bayonet in a frog. The large pack or knapsack on the back was of blackened canvas reinforced with wooden slats and bound along the bottom and corners with leather. In the centre of the pack was painted the regimental badge or number. The pack was borne on 2 white buff straps passing round the arms at the shoulder and joined across the chest by another strap to keep it in position. On the pack were the blanket and the D-shaped mess-tin in a black oilskin cover. (The D-shaped mess-tin was probably the longest issued piece of military equipment. Introduced in 1817, it was still used by some colonial troops as late as 1944.) A white canvas haversack and round wooden water-bottle completed the outfit. The belt holding the bayonet was fastened on the chest with a regimental-pattern crossbelt plate. These varied from 1800 to 1850.

In 1850 improved equipment was introduced, but because of the usual delay in implementing new issues did not become universal until about 1854–55. This replaced the bayonet frog belt and the one fastened by the ornamental beltplate with a single waist-belt with brass locket.

As general issue by 1855, the equipment consisted of one white crossbelt holding the large ammunition pouch, which was now slightly smaller, and a waist-belt with bayonet frog. Another black leather ammunition box or pouch was fitted on the right front of the waist-belt, but issued only for active service. On the crossbelt was a small white buff pouch for percussion caps. The remainder of the equipment was worn as previously. In 1856 the knapsack was reduced in size and the chest connecting strap discontinued.

This equipment continued in use with the addition in 1860 of a new pattern white leather pouch to be worn on the waist-belt in place of the black one. In 1868 experiments were conducted with a new pattern, and on 1 July the Royal Marines at Plymouth received 40 sets for issue on trial to selected N.C.O.s and men. The new pattern was approved, and valise equipment superseded knapsacks in the Royal Marines on 17 January 1870 and in the 2nd Battalion Rifle Brigade on 1 February. The new equipment was designed for even distribution of weight, most of which was borne on the shoulder straps. Contemporary photographs show that it consisted of a waist-belt, 2 divided cross braces, a bayonet frog, 2 black leather pouches and the black valise with mess-tin, blanket, haversack and water-bottle. Except for Guards and the 29th Foot pouches were of black leather until c. 1880. The Guards and the 29th Foot had white pouches, the latter adopting them in 1877. Black pouches, however, were used by Commonwealth and Dominion troops for some time. The cross straps fastened to the waist-belt at the front, passed over the shoulders, crossed at the back and fastened back to the braces at the front. The valise, resting on the buttocks with the blanket rolled above, was attached to the brass rings at the front on the braces. An expense pouch in black leather carried on the belt at the front hung below the right pouch on the belt. When the valise was not worn the expense pouch suspended from the intersection of the braces by a white buff strap. In 1882 improved valise equipment was introduced. This remained basically the same, but with a new pattern of valise worn higher at the back. An entrenching tool was issued for a short time with the new equipment. Pouches were now white. In 1888 the Slade Wallace equipment, designed by Colonel Slade and Lieutenant-Colonel Wallace, was introduced. This consisted of a waist-belt, 2 pouches and 2 cross braces which passed over the shoulders, crossed and fastened back to the belt. A new pattern of valise was introduced, now carried high on the shoulders, fastening to the cross braces with a strap held by the brass D on the shoulder and engaging the double brass buckle on the front of the brace. Below the valise was the mess-tin in oilskin cover and rolled blanket attached to the belt. Various patterns of pouch were tried with this equipment. The expense pouch of the valise equipment was abandoned, and for a short time a 10-round magazine was issued for the rifle and worn on the left brace in a small pouch above the ammunition pouch. This is shown in contemporary photographs and Simkin prints. (R. Simkin was a noted military artist whose prints were widespread during the first quarter of the twentieth century.) Once again the issue took time, though the pouches were issued to those with the old equipment because of the change of ammunition. Volunteer units were supplied last; some in fact were awaiting the valise equipment.

So diverse was that of the London Volunteers that a 'Patriotic Volunteer Fund' was instigated by Sir James Whitehead, the Lord Mayor, to assist commanding officers to complete the equipment of their regiments. The History of the 17th North Middlesex Rifle Volunteers stated 'this was well entertained and liberally supported, resulting eventually in the "Slade Wallace" and other such equipment being wholly or in part provided to various regiments'.

On active service various regiments dyed or stained their equipment with tea or coffee to give it a darkish colour.

After the Boer War in 1903 the short magazine Lee-Enfield rifle (S.M.L.E.) was introduced. This featured charger loading (the bullets were in clips and not single rounds). To facilitate carrying ammunition in the clips a new pattern of equipment in brown leather with brass buckles was authorised. It consisted of a waist-belt with 4 pouches, 2 either side. Worn over the left shoulder was a brown leather bandolier with 5 pouches. A bayonet frog was worn on the left side on the belt, although the 1903 pattern bayonet had a frog integral with the scabbard. A pack and rolled blanket were carried on the back, and a water-bottle and haversack on each hip from independent cross-straps.

Although superseded in 1908 by woven webbing equipment, some regiments were still using the older type during the landings at Gallipoli in 1915.

The webbing equipment introduced in 1908 consisted of a wide web belt with a slide brass buckle at the front and 2 buckles and short straps at the back. At the front 2 straight cross straps were fitted behind the set of 5 pouches arranged two over three. The straps crossed at the back and fastened to the buckles at the back of the waist-belt. A large pack was worn on the back, strapped to the cross straps on the shoulder. Water-bottle and haversack were buckled to the free ends of the cross straps. A bayonet frog was worn on the left side and an entrenching tool cover at the back.

During the First World War a version of the Slade Wallace equipment was made in leather and issued to Territorial and African Troops.

After the end of the First World War the 1908 equipment remained, and the issue was extended to cover all British, Dominion and Empire troops. This equipment was superseded by the introduction of the 1937 pattern, which consisted of a web belt with 2 large pouches either side designed to hold 3 Bren-gun magazines or a 50-round canvas bandolier. There were 2 braces, shaped wide where they passed over the shoulders, attached at the front and crossing at the back before buckling on to the belt. A small pack was carried on the left and a water-bottle on the right, buckled to the strap ends. A large pack was carried on the shoulders, and the straps which passed round the shoulders clipped on to brass Ds on the braces to keep it in place. A bayonet frog was carried on the belt on the left side. This equipment was worn throughout the 1939–45 engagement.

NOTE

From 1868 until 1908 various Dominion and Empire countries, particularly Indian Army regiments, sometimes adopted their own modifications or pattern.

APPENDIX 4

Number	Title Pre-1881	Title 1881
1st Ft.	The Royal Scots	The Lothian Regt.
2nd Ft.	The Queen's Royal	The Queen's (Royal West Surrey Regt.)
3rd Ft.	East Kent (The Buffs)	The Buffs (East Kent Regt.)
4th Ft.	The King's Own	The King's Own (Royal Lancaster Regt.)
5th Ft.	Northumberland (Fusiliers)	The Northumberland Fusiliers
6th Ft.	Royal First Warwickshire	Royal Warwickshire Regt.
7th Ft.	Royal Fusiliers	Royal Fusiliers (City of London Regt.)
8th Ft.	The King's	Liverpool Regt.
9th Ft.	East Norfolk	Norfolk Regt.
10th Ft.	North Lincoln	Lincolnshire Regt.
11th Ft.	North Devon	Devonshire Regt.
12th Ft.	East Suffolk	Suffolk Regt.
13th Ft.	1st Somersetshire (Prince Albert's Regt. of Light Infantry)	The Prince Albert's (Somersetshire Light Infantry)
14th Ft.	Buckinghamshire or Prince of Wales' Own	The Prince of Wales' Own (West Yorkshire Regt.)
15th Ft.	York East Riding	East Yorkshire Regt.
16th Ft.	Bedfordshire	Bedfordshire Regt.
17th Ft.	Leicestershire	Leicestershire Regt.
18th Ft.	Royal Irish	Royal Irish Regt.
19th Ft.	1st York North Riding Princess of Wales' Own	Princess of Wales' Own (Yorkshire Regt.)
20th Ft.	East Devonshire	Lancashire Fusiliers
21st Ft.	Royal Scots Fusiliers	Royal Scots Fusiliers
22nd Ft.	Cheshire	Cheshire Regt.
23rd Ft.	Royal Welch Fusiliers	Royal Welch Fusiliers
24th Ft.	2nd Warwickshire	South Wales Borderers
25th Ft.	King's Own Borderers	King's Own Borderers
26th Ft.	Cameronians	1st Btn. Cameronians (Scottish Rifles)
27th Ft.	Inniskilling	1st Btn. Royal Inniskilling Fusiliers

Number	Title Pre-1881	Title 1881
28th Ft.	North Gloucestershire	1st Btn. Gloucestershire Regt.
29th Ft.	Worcestershire	1st Btn. Worcestershire Regt.
30th Ft.	Cambridgeshire	1st Btn. East Lancashire Regt.
31st Ft.	Huntingdonshire	1st Btn. East Surrey Regt.
32nd Ft.	Cornwall Light Infantry	1st Btn. Duke of Cornwall's Light Infantry
33rd Ft.	Duke of Wellington's	1st Btn. Duke of Wellington's (West Riding Regt.)
34th Ft.	Cumberland	1st Btn. Border Regt.
35th Ft.	Royal Sussex	1st Btn. Royal Sussex Regt.
36th Ft.	Herefordshire	2nd Btn. Worcestershire Regt.
37th Ft.	North Hampshire	1st Btn. Hampshire Regt.
38th Ft.	1st Staffordshire	1st Btn. South Staffordshire Regt.
39th Ft.	Dorsetshire	1st Btn. Dorsetshire Regt.
40th Ft.	2nd Somersetshire	1st Btn. Prince of Wales's Volunteers (South Lancashire Regt.)
41st Ft.	Welsh	1st Btn. Welsh Regt.
42nd Ft.	Royal Highland (Black Watch)	1st Btn. Black Watch (Royal Highlanders)
43rd Ft.	Monmouthshire Light Infantry	1st Btn. Oxfordshire Light Infantry
44th Ft.	East Sussex	1st Btn. Essex Regt.
45th Ft.	Nottinghamshire Sherwood Foresters	1st Btn. Sherwood Foresters (Derbyshire) Regt.
46th Ft.	South Devonshire	2nd Btn. Duke of Cornwall's Light Infantry
47th Ft.	Lancashire	1st Btn. Loyal North Lancashire Regt.
48th Ft.	Northamptonshire	1st Btn. Northamptonshire Regt.
49th Ft.	Princess Charlotte of Wales' or Hertfordshire	1st Btn. Princess Charlotte of Wales' (Berkshire Regt.)
50th Ft.	Queen's Own	1st Btn. Queen's Own (Royal West Kent Regt.)
51st Ft.	2nd Yorkshire, West Riding or The King's Own Light Infantry	1st Btn. The King's Own Light Infantry (South Yorkshire Regt.)
52nd Ft.	Oxfordshire Light Infantry	2nd Btn. Oxfordshire Light Infantry

Number	Title Pre-1881	Title 1881
53rd Ft.	Shropshire	1st Btn. The King's Light Infantry (Shropshire Regt.)
54th Ft.	West Norfolk	2nd Btn. Dorsetshire Regt.
55th Ft.	Westmorland	2nd Btn. Border Regt.
56th Ft.	West Essex	2nd Btn. Essex Regt.
57th Ft.	West Middlesex	1st Btn. Duke of Cambridge's Own (Middlesex Regt.)
58th Ft.	Rutlandshire	2nd Btn. Northamptonshire Regt.
59th Ft.	2nd Nottinghamshire	2nd Btn. East Lancashire Regt.
60th Ft.	King's Royal Rifle Corps	King's Royal Rifle Corps
61st Ft.	South Gloucestershire	2nd Btn. Gloucestershire Regt.
62nd Ft.	Wiltshire	1st Btn. Duke of Edinburgh's (Wiltshire Regt.)
63rd Ft.	West Suffolk	1st Btn. Manchester Regt.
64th Ft.	2nd Staffordshire	1st Btn. Prince of Wales' (North Staffordshire Regt.)
65th Ft.	2nd Yorkshire North Riding	1st Btn. York & Lancaster Regt.
66th Ft.	Berkshire	2nd Btn. Princess Charlotte of Wales' (Berkshire Regt.)
67th Ft.	South Hampshire	2nd Btn. Hampshire Regt.
68th Ft.	Durham Light Infantry	1st Btn. Durham Light Infantry
69th Ft.	South Lincolnshire	2nd Btn. Welsh Regt.
70th Ft.	Surrey	2nd Btn. East Surrey Regt.
71st Ft.	Highland Light Infantry	1st Btn. Highland Light Infantry
72nd Ft.	Duke of Albany's Own Highlanders	1st Btn. Seaforth Highlanders (Ross-shire Buffs, The Duke of Albany's)
73rd Ft.	Perthshire	2nd Btn. Black Watch (Royal Highlanders)
74th Ft.	Highlanders	2nd Btn. Highland Light Infantry
75th Ft.	Stirlingshire	1st Btn. Gordon Highlanders
76th Ft.	No Title	2nd Btn. The Duke of Wellington's (West Riding Regt.)
77th Ft.	East Middlesex or Duke of Cambridge's Own	2nd Btn. Duke of Cambridge's Own (Middlesex Regt.)

Number	Title Pre-1881	Title 1881
78th Ft.	Highland or Ross-shire Buffs	2nd Btn. Seaforth Highlanders (Ross-shire Buffs, The Duke of Albany's)
79th Ft.	Queen's Own Cameron Highlanders	Queen's Own Cameron Highlanders
80th Ft.	Staffordshire Volunteers	2nd Btn. South Staffordshire Regt.
81st Ft.	Loyal Lincoln Volunteers	2nd Btn. Loyal North Lancashire Regt.
82nd Ft.	Prince of Wales' Volunteers	2nd Btn. Prince of Wales' Volunteers (South Lanca- Regt.)
83rd Ft.	County of Dublin	1st Btn. Royal Irish Rifles
84th Ft.	York & Lancaster	2nd Btn. York & Lancaster Regt.
85th Ft.	King's Light Infantry	2nd Btn. The King's Light Infantry (Shropshire Regt.)
86th Ft.	Royal County Down	2nd Btn. Royal Irish Rifles
87th Ft.	Royal Irish Fusiliers	1st Btn. Princess Victoria's (Royal Irish Fusiliers)
88th Ft.	Connaught Rangers	1st Btn. Connaught Rangers
89th Ft.	Princess Victoria's	2nd Btn. Princess Victoria's (Royal Irish Fusiliers)
90th Ft.	Perthshire Volunteers Light Infantry	2nd Btn. Cameronians (Scottish Rifles)
91st Ft.	Princess Louise's Argyllshire Highlanders	1st Btn. Princess Louise's (Sutherland and Argyll Highlanders)
92nd Ft.	Gordon Highlanders	2nd Btn. Gordon Highlanders
93rd Ft.	Sutherland Highlanders	2nd Btn. Princess Louise's (Sutherland and Argyll Highlanders)
94th Ft.	No Title	2nd Btn. Connaught Rangers
95th Ft.	Derbyshire	2nd Btn. Sherwood Foresters (Derbyshire Regt.)
96th Ft.	No Title	2nd Btn. Manchester Regt.
97th Ft.	Earl of Ulster's	2nd Btn. Queen's Own (Royal West Kent Regt.)
98th Ft.	Prince of Wales'	2nd Btn. Prince of Wales' (North Staffordshire Regt.)
99th Ft.	Duke of Edinburgh's	2nd Btn. Duke of Edinburgh's (Wiltshire Regt.)

Number	Title Pre-1881	Title 1881
100th Ft.	Prince of Wales' Royal Canadian	1st Btn. Prince of Wales' Leinster Regt. (Royal Canadians)
101st Ft.	101st Royal Bengal Fusiliers	1st Btn. Royal Munster Fusiliers
102nd Ft.	102nd Royal Madras Fusiliers	1st Btn. Royal Dublin Fusiliers
103rd Ft.	103rd Royal Bombay Fusiliers	2nd Btn. Royal Dublin Fusiliers
104th Ft.	104th Bengal Fusiliers	2nd Btn. Royal Munster Fusiliers
105th Ft.	105th Madras Light Infantry	2nd Btn. King's Own Light Infantry (South Yorkshire Regt.)
106th Ft.	106th Bombay Light Infantry	2nd Btn. Durham Light Infantry
107th Ft.	107th Bengal Infantry	2nd Btn. Royal Sussex Regt.
108th Ft.	108th Madras Infantry	2nd Btn. Royal Inniskilling Fusiliers
109th Ft.	109th Bombay Infantry	2nd Btn. Prince of Wales' Leinster Regt. (Royal Canadians)
	Prince Consort's Own (Rifle Brigade)	Rifle Brigade (Prince Consort's Own)

SELECT BIBLIOGRAPHY

WEAPONS

Blackmore, H. L., *British Military Firearms*. Jenkins, 1961
Hutchinson, Lt.-Col., *Machine Guns*. Macmillan, 1938
Reynolds, E. G. B., *The Lee-Enfield Rifle*. Jenkins, 1960.
Roads, C. H., *British Soldiers' Firearms 1850–1864*. Jenkins, 1964
Wilkinson-Latham, J., *British Military Swords*. Hutchinson, 1966
Wilkinson-Latham, R., *British Military Bayonets 1700–1945*. Hutchinson, 1967

UNIFORMS

Carman, W. Y., *Indian Army Uniforms*, Vol. 2 Infantry. Morgan-Grampian, 1969; *British Military Uniforms*. Longacre Press, 1962.
Cooper King, C., *The British Army and Auxiliary Forces*. Cassell, 1893
Luard, J., *History of Dress of the British Soldier*. William Clowes, 1852
Milne, S. M., *Standards and Colours of the Army*. Privately Printed, 1893
Navy and Army Illustrated. Newnes, 1895 *et seq.*
Parkyn, H. G., *Shoulder, Belt Plates and Buttons*. Gale and Polden, 1956
Richards, W., *His Majesty's Territorial Army*, Vols. 1–4. Virtue. (Date unknown.)
Wilkinson-Latham, R. and C., *Infantry Uniforms, 1742-1855* Blandford, 1969

Also numerous regimental histories and photographs in the authors' and other collections.

INDEX